THE SPIRITUAL SIDE OF DISABILITY

THE LIGHTSEEKER'S WAY TO THRIVE WITH A
SPECIAL NEEDS CHILD

HELENA CLARE

Copyright © 2021 by HELENA CLARE
All rights reserved.

No part of this publication may be reproduced, stored in a retrieval system, or transmitted in any form or by any means, electronic, mechanical, scanning, recording, photocopying, or otherwise, without the prior written permission of the author.

Limit of Liability/Disclaimer of Warranty: This publication is designed to provide accurate and authoritative information in regard to the subject matter covered. It is sold with the understanding that neither the author nor the publisher is engaged in rendering legal, investment, accounting or other professional services. While the publisher and author have used their best efforts in preparing this book, they make no representations or warranties with respect to the accuracy or completeness of the contents of this book and specifically disclaim any implied warranties of merchantability or fitness for a particular purpose. No warranty may be created or extended by sales representatives or written sales materials. The advice and strategies contained herein may not be suitable for your situation. You should consult with a professional when appropriate. Neither the publisher nor the author shall be liable for any loss of profit or any other commercial damages, including but not limited to special, incidental, consequential, personal, or other damages.

THE SPIRITUAL SIDE OF DISABILITY
The Lightseeker's Way to Thrive With a Special Needs Child
By HELENA CLARE
1. FAM012000 2. SEL032000 3. OCC032000
ISBN: 978-1-949642-51-3
EBOOK: 978-1-949642-52-0

Cover design by LEWIS AGRELL

Printed in the United States of America

Authority Publishing
11230 Gold Express Dr. #310-413
Gold River, CA 95670
800-877-1097
www.AuthorityPublishing.com

This book is dedicated to my beautiful son Saafi,
who lights up the world and who I love dearly.

Contents

Our Blue Roses 11

Chapter 1: My Story 17

Chapter 2: Getting Started 29
   Preparing for a Visualisation...............................30
   Grounding and Protection 30
   A Word on Unwanted Spirit Guests 33
   Getting the Purest Message.................................33

Chapter 3: The Emotional Rollercoaster 36
   Shock and Denial 39
   Anger Towards Myself...41
   Anger from a Mate..44
   Control..45
   Fear and Anxiety...47
   Depression and Feeling Overwhelmed..................49
   Acceptance and Finding the Platinum Lining ...52

Chapter 4: Soul Contracts & Our Purpose as
Humans On Earth 57
   Soul Contracts 58

Exercise: Finding Patterns in Your Life 59
Karma..60
Accepting and Letting Go 61
A Word on Death..61
Finding Your Soul Purpose...............................64
✦*Visualisation to Understand the Soul
Contracts with Your Disabled Children*✦ 65
✦*Visualisation: Understanding Your Life Purpose*✦ 66

Chapter 5: The Heart of Well-Being 69
Spirituality and Personal Development........................72
Nurturing Yourself..74
Exercise: Making Vows to Yourself............................78

Chapter 6: Career & Finances 82

Chapter 7: Health 87
✦*Visualisation to Connect with a Dis-eased
Body Part*✦ 91

Chapter 8: Finding the Platinum Lining 93
Giving Thanks...94
Giving Back..95
Colour..96

Chapter 9: The Power Of Words..................99
The Power of Thoughts 102
The Ego..103
Unconditional Love and the Self..............................105
✦*Visualisation to Bring in Unconditional Love
with Lady Gaia*✦ 109
Exercise: Learning to Love Yourself 110

Chapter 10: Family & Friends.....................113
Remembering Your Other Children 114
Your Children's Relationship with Each Other...............116
Allow Your Able-Bodied Children to Be Carefree..........117
Relationships..118

A Stronger Relationship 118
Finding a New Special Other..119
Knowing When to Let Go 120

Chapter 11: Drainers & Energisers 122
*Exercise: Developing Your Relationship Map
and Top Five Actions* 122
Drainers..124
Energisers 126
Letting Go of a Draining Relationship........................127
✺*Visualisation to Help with Difficult Decisions*✺ 128
Interpreting the Visualisation 130
✺*Visualisation: Letting Go of a Draining
Relationship, with the Help of Archangel Michael*✺....131

Chapter 12: Dealing with Negative Emotions 133
Energetic Defence Mechanisms....................................133
Guilt, Fear and Anger 136
Exercise: Identifying Guilt 137
✺*Visualisation to Release Guilt with Archangel
Chamuel*✺ 137
✺*Visualisation to Let Go of Anger*✺ 139
✺*Visualisation to Release Fear with Ray o' Light*✺ 141

**Chapter 13: Creating Hope Through New
Technologies** 143
✺*Visualisation to Bring New Technologies into
Your Life*✺ 144

Chapter 14: Setting Goals 147
Honing In on Your Goals 147
*Exercise: Use Your Conscious Mind to Identify
Your Goals*...148
Exercise: Channelling Your Goals 148
Goal Helpers & Goal Teams..152

Conclusion: Bringing It All Together 156

Checklist..156
Incorporating spirituality into your daily life:...............157

Free Printable Pdfs 159

Connect On Social Media 160

Appendix 1: Angels & Divine Messages 161
How are divine messages received? 162
What is so special about a Guardian Angel? 163
What are the Archangels?..163
What are Ascended Masters? 164

Appendix 2: Understanding Chakras...........................165
How Chakras Relate to Our Spiritual Path..................168
Archangels and Chakras 170

Appendix 3: Other Celestial Tools................................172
The Golden, Silver, Violet Flame...................................172
The Christ Consciousness Energy...................................173

Appendix 4: The Kahunas..174

Appendix 5: Colours And The Archangels....................177

About Helena Clare..182

Free Meditation..184

Acknowledgements..185

Photo 1: Saafi and his mum Helena

Our Blue Roses

I am clairaudient, which means I can hear voices from the spirit world as clearly as a person sitting next to me. I met my Guardian Angel when I was about sixteen and since then have been blessed to meet countless Archangels, ascended masters and other wise beings from the celestial kingdom (the name I give to the place where God and spirits of a certain level of purity reside).

Over the years I've learnt there is not one single religion that is the truth - the truth is bigger, embracing all religions and approaches to life that seek goodness and acceptance.

In 2011 I started receiving messages directly from Source, God or whatever you choose to call the Creator. This relationship has strengthened my resilience and also given me insight into the reason I've been gifted a 'special' child.

Source has now asked me to write this book, to explain the soul contracts we agree with our loved ones before we are born, and how powerful the souls of disabled children and adults often are. This book is relevant to parents of physically and mentally disabled children of any level of severity. It is also relevant to parents of children with a terminal illness or serious medical condition.

In many communities in the world, disability is a taboo. In some places, mentally and/or physically disabled children are not accepted - even being chained to tables, kept in cages and abandoned or killed. One of the most moving videos I have seen in my career was of an Asian village decimated by a cyclone, where a deaf child was filmed chained inside a cage. Fortunately the cage was intact and the boy alive, but can you imagine the fear of a deaf child or a disabled child unable to run or hide because they have been imprisoned due to their disability. We *need* to change how we think about disability in the world, and I hope this book plays some role in effecting that change.

Part of this book's aim is to communicate the message that disabled children are *special* children, often very evolved souls given to us as gifts to help our own ascension and that of those around them. Rather than pity them or resent them, we should celebrate their bravery as souls in this life, give thanks that we have been given them, and do our best to learn the soul lessons and life path they have agreed to help us reach.

That is not to downplay how tough and challenging it can be to see our children suffer or (in our perception) miss out on the opportunities able-bodied and minded children have. It is also not to ignore how difficult it can be to parent a disabled child, managing stigma and physical and emotional challenges, especially if we have limited money and support from others. But the spiritual path with our children is about finding the joy and the platinum lining of this soul bond.

A wise Muslim *imam* gave me a wonderful poem that celebrates our special children. The poem calls these children 'Blue Roses'. It is moving and insightful, and I would like to share it here.

I AM A BLUE ROSE

I am the blue rose of life
rare and unique as
summer snow
glistening in the morning sun
admired by
hearts and souls each day.
I also have a share in the
Garden of Life.
I am your teacher.
If you allow me,
I will teach you what is really important
in life.
I will give you and teach you unconditional love.
I gift you with my innocent trust, my dependency upon you.
I teach you about how precious this life is
and about not taking things for granted.
I teach you about forgetting your own needs, desires and dreams.
I give you opportunities,
opportunities to discover the depth of your character,
not mine.
The depth of your love, your commitment, your patience, your abilities.
The opportunity to explore your spirit more deeply.

*I drive you further than you would ever
   go on your own,
working harder,
seeking answers to your many questions
   with no answers.
I teach you giving
Most of all I teach you hope and faith.
I am your 'Blue Rose'.*

'Blue Roses are rare, special and are adored by everyone. The Blue Rose symbolizes our "CHILDREN OF HEAVEN", rare, unique and beautiful, meriting the love and affection of all.' Reference: www.radioislam.co.za

One point worth emphasizing is that the book you are reading, *The Spiritual Side of Disability*, is not about *getting by* - it is about *thriving*.

I love the concept of resilience. To be resilient is not just to withstand a shock. It is about bouncing back stronger and more vibrant than before – thriving in the face of adversity.

It has amused and at times bewildered me that during the first three years of Saafi's life, in my international development career, I was working on how to build resilience in poor communities in Africa and Asia. One of my roles was to prioritise projects for funding that were likely to make the greatest contribution to the resilience of communities vulnerable to droughts, flooding, and other natural disasters. I hadn't spent time thinking about the concept of resilience before I started this role. However, I read extensively and understood how catastrophic events like an earthquake or massive flood can break one city for decades after, leaving it with higher crime rates, social strife, and poorer health and education results, whilst another city might use the catastrophe to build stronger relationship bonds between its residents and to restructure itself as a more vibrant place to live than before, with improved social and environmental indicators. An inspiring book to read on this subject is Judith Rodin's *The Resilience Dividend,* which explores human resilience in the face of climate and other shocks to cities and communities.

Just like the city of Tulsa, Oklahoma used the devastating flood of 1984 to invest in long-term planning for prevention and recovery, and came together as a community, we can become more resilient in the face of shocks. One of the things I have realised is that with a severely disabled child like my beautiful son, there is not one traumatic episode that you weather and then it's smooth sailing. Traumatic events may become part of the normal, and you have to get used to that. Similarly, parenting a child with a terminal illness may have sunny spells, but one has to cope with the reality of deteriorating health and death. Rather than a smooth decline, there may be sudden setbacks that require fortitude to withstand.

It may take some time, but through working with the exercises in this book you will become more resilient - you will become stronger and more vibrant and more aligned with your highest purpose and potential in life.

To thrive or become more resilient, we have to:

a) look for the platinum lining (even better than a silver lining),
b) accept and let go, and
c) ensure that, as parents, we love and nurture ourselves.

Throughout this book, you will find spiritual explanation, guided meditations and exercises to help you realise your full potential through our 'special children', so we can give them the greatest gift in our possession: our own happiness and fulfilment.

I send you love and wish you bravery and resilience on this journey with our beautiful children. It is for us to find the platinum lining in our storm clouds.

Chapter 1
MY STORY

It is 1:40 am on a humid Sunday morning. I am lying in bed, in a private women's and babies' hospital in Pretoria, South Africa. I am a continent away from my parents and my birthplace of Cornwall, England. Forty hours ago I gave birth to a beautiful baby boy weighing 2.4kg, who now lies beside me in a cot. He is called Saafi, an Arabic word, meaning pure, clear, crystal. It's the name he told me he wanted when he was still in my womb.

Saafi hasn't suckled yet. He has hardly made a sound since he was born. Two jolly African nurses have sat either side of me, milking my breasts like a cow to get the colostrum out, so every few hours he has had some nutrition. I'm not worried…yet.

The door opens, casting bright light from the corridor into my darkened room. It's the doctor with some assistants. The doctor wears a white hospital coat and holds a clipboard, flicking through some papers on it. She stands just inside the doorway, so her notes are lit from the passage light.

'He has to be admitted to ICU, now', she says to me through the darkness.

'What? Why?' I ask.

'The blood sugar is low'.

I start to protest, not understanding why she wants to take my baby away.

The doctor explains. 'If his blood sugar drops below a certain threshold, there is a risk his brain can be damaged. He's not at that point yet, but I don't want to take that risk.'

Of course I don't argue. One of the assistants scoops up my son in a bundle of swaddling blanket. Saafi doesn't make a sound.

'You can sit with him in ICU', the doctor says, 'but he also has jaundice, so he'll be under lights. You won't be able to hold him'.

The small group exits the room. I dress swiftly, without a care for my unkempt look, and run through the details of the birth that is still fresh in my mind and body. It took me a long time to go into labour after my waters broke, I think around twenty-seven hours. But Saafi was monitored in my womb by the midwife and didn't show any sign of distress. The midwife discovered during the course of the night that a water bubble above Saafi's head was blocking his descent into the birth canal. Once that was popped, active labour quickly ensued.

Saafi's father and I had chosen a luxury birthing room annexed to the hospital. Run by midwives, it was like a comfortable hotel room, with a double bed, soft candles, colourful padded chairs and a large, free-standing birthing bath.

Once I was in active labour, birth took just over three hours. I used the positive affirmation, 'I will have a smooth, swift, safe labour of less than four hours, throughout my pregnancy'. It had worked with my first-born, Tariq, who had also predicted the date and time of his birth to within 15 minutes.

Being clairaudient means that whilst I can hear the voices of angels and God, I have also enjoyed hearing the voices of my two boys before they were conceived, and then during pregnancy. It's just like having a conversation with a friend who is sitting beside me, except the voice beams straight into my mind. With Tariq I had checked in on him on a daily basis, asking how he was and whether he needed anything or wanted me to do anything differently.

On that occasion, it was about 10 days before my due date and my husband and I had been invited to a party at a friend's house on Saturday night. Another friend had asked me to help her move house on Sunday. The conversation went like this:

> 'Hi Tariq, is it okay if I go to Ade and Anna's party this weekend?'
>
> 'Yes mum that's fine', the voice responded, 'just for a couple hours'.
>
> 'And then would it be okay to help Fatima pack some of her boxes on Sunday?'
>
> 'Sorry, no, Mum. On Sunday you need to rest and stay at home'.
>
> 'Oh, really?' I asked, surprised. 'Why? Are you coming soon?'
>
> 'Yes, Mum, I'll be with you around 8am on Monday'.

He arrived at 0815.

Saafi had been equally communicative and warned me the day my 'plug' was going to shed. It was Eid Al-Adha, the second of two holy days celebrated in the Islamic calendar, equivalent to Christmas for Muslims. Saafi was two weeks off his due date. My husband was Muslim and we liked to go to his sister's house for Eid. She lived in a suburb of Johannesburg, a good one-hour drive from Pretoria, where we lived. We'd planned to go to her house as usual, but I checked in with Saafi, just to be sure. The answer came back a clear, 'No, Mum, you need to rest and prepare for me. I'm coming soon.' That night, my waters broke.

Towards the end of labour, Saafi didn't seem to want to come out. My midwife asked me what was holding me back. Was I worried about anything? In her extensive experience, if a birthing mother had a fear, this could inhibit the progression of the birth. I said I was worried he was going to be brain-damaged.

Getting that shocking thought verbally out of my body - a thought that had been ever-present since Saafi had warned me, just before a scare in the early part of my pregnancy - seemed to allow my body to open. My little Saafi literally launched into the water bath like a blueish-red torpedo and was placed into my arms by the midwife.

Shortly after, the umbilical cord was cut and Saafi was taken to a side table to be weighed and have his APGAR score taken. This simple test is used in hospitals to assess a newborn baby's health and risk of mortality. The test includes checking the baby's:

- Appearance
- Pulse (heart rate)

- Grimace response (reflexes)
- Activity (muscle tone)
- Respiration

Saafi's score was within the normal range, so I was confounded now that the doctors had whisked Saafi away to ICU. If the APGAR score had been above 7 out of 10 only the day before, indicating a healthy child, why was Saafi suddenly being rushed to intensive care? Why was my healthy newborn now suffering low blood sugar? He hadn't suckled directly from me, but we'd painfully squeezed teaspoonfuls of colostrum from my nipples. Surely that had been enough. Should I have woken him more often? And hadn't the nurses been coming at routine intervals to milk me like a cow? That's what it had felt like.

As mentioned, Saafi had spoken to me throughout the pregnancy. After 'the scare', he'd told me that as long as I did enough deep breathing exercises he should be fine, and should get enough oxygen. But what if he was just trying to protect me from the reality?

I phone my husband to let him know Saafi is going into the ICU. I'm sure he'll come down immediately, so we can face this setback together. Two are stronger than one.

But when I get through, having let the phone ring for what seems like an age, he says he will visit in the morning. The morning! His sister Zaitoon is there, so she can stay with Tariq in the house. It's a short 7-minute drive by car. There won't be any traffic at this time of night. How can he not want to come? What father would not want to come? He rings off.

Bewildered, I make my way to the intensive care ward for babies - alone.

I ring the intercom to be let in. In some ways, this is a doorway into a very personal hell. This first night is like being at the top step of hell. In the following three weeks, things keep getting worse, and I descend further and further into the abyss.

***

Looking back, it's hard to believe I wasn't in that ICU for several years. I remember every sensation of those three weeks, punctuated by harrowing images.

On the first night, Saafi was put on an I.V. drip and placed under lights to treat him for jaundice. The ward was mostly full of premature babies, so Saafi was one of the bigger ones. The staff were warm, motherly, attentive to the children; the air was cool and clinical. I couldn't touch Saafi; he was in his own little insulated world. It all felt rather unreal. But I wasn't too worried at that stage. Jaundice isn't uncommon and his blood sugar would be addressed by the drip.

I kept to a strict breast milk expressing regime, which went something like this: ICU 1.5 hours, express in my hospital room for 45 minutes, rest for 45 minutes and repeat the cycle again. Saafi's father would pop in now and again, but our five-year-old Tariq, desperate to be with his new brother, was too young to be allowed in the ICU, much to his chagrin.

On the second night, things became more nightmarish. Shocked to find Saafi wasn't in his usual place, I asked a nurse where I could find him. The nurse guided me to a different part of the ward. Saafi was now rigged up to an oxygen monitor and heartbeat monitor, along with the drip and tubes up his nose. A nurse was perched by the side of his bed.

'What's going on?' I asked her.

'He keeps forgetting to breathe. So when he does, I wake him up'.

He keeps forgetting to breathe! The words rang in my head. He looked pathetic with all the tubes coming out of him. He still hadn't made a noise, even though he was regularly pricked for bloods. He just seemed to sleep.

I sat down heavily. I felt incredibly alone. My friends and family called and messaged frequently, but I couldn't think beyond: express milk, see Saafi, drag myself through the day. I am a naturally positive person, but I couldn't even hold my baby. It all felt weird and wrong. My mum wanted to fly out immediately, but she had just had an eye operation and it seemed more sensible for her to come after we had been discharged, as she would only have a limited amount of time to stay in the country.

Over the next three weeks, Saafi was tested for pretty much everything. He had a lumbar puncture, which involved a large needle inserted into his spine. He was given antibiotics even though he showed no sign of infection. Blood test after blood test was taken and all came back without a shred of insight.

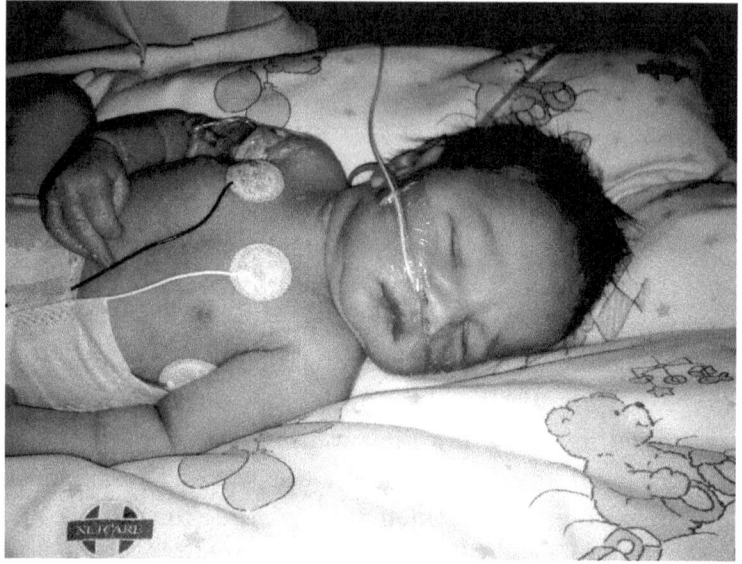

Photo 2: Saafi in Intensive Care

Eventually, an ambulance transported us - with Saafi in an incubator - to another hospital. In some ways we had the royal treatment. He was high-risk so we had several paramedics with us. I remember the ambulance driver, a black South African, complaining about the renaming of all the street names in Pretoria, done to purge the apartheid history in the country. Perhaps done overzealously, leaving many people lost with obsolete maps. Why Church Street had to be renamed, I will never understand; everyone goes to church whatever their race. He said it was a nightmare trying to find their way around in an emergency.

We arrived at the new hospital and were escorted to a reception room with more friendly, understanding people. They brought us into the radiology department, where an MRI scan was done on Saafi's brain. The MRI was a massive, clunking, weird machine. It's hard to describe just how horribly noisy and loud it is, to anyone who hasn't been in one. Yet throughout this hour-long experience - or that's what it felt like - Saafi still didn't make a sound.

Soon after, Saafi's father and I were called to a gloomy hospital reminiscent of Gotham City, where we met with one of the few neurologists in Pretoria. He was reputedly very good, but his bedside manner was chilling.

He told us abruptly that Saafi's brain was damaged, specifically the thalamus, which controls all physical ability, as well as speech and concentration. He said this had been caused by medical negligence, that we should put Saafi in an institution, move on and have another child. His prognosis was that Saafi would be severely disabled, unlikely to walk or talk.

My husband dropped me off at the hospital that day. I remember sitting on my narrow single bed in the hospital visitors' ward, sobbing into my mobile phone, to my mum in Cornwall: 'I don't want a vegetable for a child.' It was a year later that I discovered the medical term for this form of brain damage: cerebral palsy.

I allowed myself to collapse emotionally in the hospital that day. How hard it must have been for my mum to hear her daughter, with that dramatic news, relayed to her from so far away, unable to reach out and hold me, hug me, like I desperately craved to be hugged.

But apart from that momentary loss of calm and a few tears over the years, I have been remarkably resilient. The reason is that I have been able to access insight, wisdom and love directly from *above*. It has given me so much strength, and I want to share this font of knowledge and love with you.

Throughout my pregnancy with Saafi and his birth - throughout the period of his trauma in ICU and the five years he has lived with us - I have continually spoken psychically with him and to my other guides in the celestial kingdom. They have given me unfaltering support, love and direction. I have spoken regularly to Saafi's higher self (his soul), to his Guardian Angel, to other celestial beings, and to Source/God directly. The message has been clear and unbending: 'Saafi is well, Saafi is a higher soul, Saafi is here to help you on your highest path, Saafi is in this world to spread light and love and to teach everyone around him. Saafi is pure. He is as pure as his name indicates: pure, clear, crystal'.

I have had many similar messages spontaneously passed to me from other psychics. I have also explored our family energetic system several times, through an alternative therapeutic technique called 'family constellations'. In this approach, people role-play the different members of a family, facilitated in a safe space. The 'role players' share whatever feelings they have and respond to the facilitator's questions as though they are the family member. I have used some 'role players' who know me well and also some who don't know me at all. With all of them, the message has been consistent.

In each situation Saafi (being role-played by an adult), far more than just being 'fine', doesn't believe there is anything wrong with him; he is completely at peace with his situation. He shows immense understanding of his parents and their weaknesses, who in contrast exhibit all sorts of limitations. In these family constellations Saafi also demonstrates an incredibly strong bond with his brother, Tariq. But he shows absolutely no concern with his physical limitations. He doesn't feel there is anything wrong with himself, although he would like to know what it feels like to walk someday.

Time has passed since we listened to that chilling news from the neurologist in the Gotham City type hospital. He was spot-on in his diagnosis. Saafi hasn't yet learnt to walk or talk at the age of almost six. But what the medical prediction of this expert failed to take into account when he recommended we put Saafi in a home, was just how much joy Saafi brings. He laughs and chuckles at jokes. I've known him to chortle for a full thirty minutes sometimes, with the antics of his brother, or his friends. And whilst my husband and I are no longer together we both adore Saafi and we have both created a family that isn't 'normal' but where we revel in the personality of Saafi, the life and vitality he brings to everyday. I also recognise that it has shaped who we are as people. I like to think it has made me stronger, and I believe it's made my eldest son a wise, nurturing person who relates to a vast range of people with care and sensitivity. It has also contributed to his wit and frivolity in life, as Saafi makes him laugh; he has also learnt that making us laugh in the hard times of Saafi's illness is a wonderful contribution he can make to his mother's happiness.

Further understanding the spiritual purpose to a child like Saafi enables a certain level of resilience in the face of challenges. Certainly, I find it challenging when he goes into hospital; each episode is an emotional rollercoaster. I also find it challenging not being able to communicate with him through speech. Understanding the spiritual lessons he brings to me and our family helps me through these times.

Knowing the profound decision at a soul level that Saafi has made by choosing this body, enables me to respect and admire him, rather than pity him. It also gives me a framework for explaining to Tariq why Saafi is the way he is. Putting Saafi in an institution, as the neurologist advised, would have meant missing out on an incredible font of joy in our lives, along with all the greater spiritual lessons.

Today Saafi is an exquisite five-year-old boy, adored by his brother and his parents. He spreads joy around him. He can't yet walk or talk. He can't sit unassisted, and he has difficulty controlling his arms and legs and lifting his head. But he can grab my hair, recognise my footsteps two rooms away, and we are training his eyes to be ready for an eye computer - in which the text on the screen is controlled by the movement of the eyes, enabling children and adults who previously couldn't communicate the ability to express themselves for the first time.

I have stopped being able to ignore a message that was increasingly frequently communicated to me by other psychics, none of whom knew each other, all echoing what my Guidance was demanding of me: that Saafi is with me for a purpose. He has been gifted to me, has chosen me at a soul level, for the message that I can help bring to the world. Saafi and so many other disabled children like him, far from being damaged, to be shunned and shrunk from, are in fact highly evolved souls, here to teach us and help us evolve faster. These children are beacons of light and love, and have a very strong, direct connection with the celestial kingdom.

Through my experience with Saafi, I know I am meant to help other parents of disabled children learn how to connect to their highest guidance, to hear, see, feel or know their angels, their spirit guides, and perhaps even to psychically communicate with their disabled children and the souls of their children.

That is why this book has been written. It is about finding your highest life purpose and the reason you've been gifted a special child. It is also about thriving with your disabled child, and finding joy, forgiveness and spiritual growth within your unique situation. I welcome you to the club of spirit power.

Chapter 2

GETTING STARTED

This book does not subscribe to a specific religion; it is all-embracing. If it is difficult for you to believe that angels or even God exists, I ask you just to enjoy the visualisations and be aware of any changes in yourself. If they make you feel good, continue with them.

Throughout my adult life, my logical brain has demanded proof of what my intuitive brain just *knows*. I've also experienced and read a wealth of evidence to support my belief system. I will never foist my beliefs on others, but I do ask you to be open-minded, so as not to shut out the incredible support and love that is within your reach.

With this in mind, this book will guide you through techniques designed to help you receive messages directly from your Guardian Angel, other archangels or wise humans who reside in the celestial kingdom. They will help you connect to your divine guidance and to thrive, understanding your life purpose on this planet and the reason you have been gifted a special child.

The techniques shared in this book are ones I have practiced and honed over the past 30 years. I've used them with classes of beginners to meditation, as well as advanced psychics. If you practise them, you will start receiving uplifting guidance and never-ending compassion, understanding and love from the highest and purest beings.

This chapter provides important notes to bear in mind as we proceed. The appendices provide additional technical detail.

Preparing for a Visualisation

Visualisation is a specific type of meditation where the mind focuses on an image or an inner journey. In the Light-Seekers Way we use visualisations to help connect to angels, as they calm the mind and make us more open to listening and receiving messages.

Before entering a visualisation it is important either to sit or lie in a symmetrical way. Some people sit cross-legged to meditate, but I find my legs go to sleep. I prefer to sit in a comfortable chair with my feet flat on the ground and my legs and arms uncrossed. I like to rest my hands palms up on my thighs, as this signals that I am open to receive information.

It's important to have a straight, aligned back rather than a slouched posture. I also love meditating lying down. It doesn't matter if you fall asleep but if you frequently fall asleep, perhaps experiment with sitting up and meditating.

Grounding and Protection

Grounding and protection are essential before commencing a visualisation.

Sometimes at the end of meditation, it is possible to feel lightheaded or even dizzy. This is because the energies we access vibrate at a cellular level, at a faster frequency than we vibrate at. This is why most of us cannot usually see angels or celestial beings.

Grounding is both a physical connection to the ground and a conscious, imagined connection with the earth. By consciously 'grounding' ourselves to the earth, we balance the light spiritual energies with our heavier physical energies.

Grounding is also important to maximise the impact of the divine messages we receive. We live in the earthly plane, and so divine messages and the power of connection to angels need to be brought into or *manifested* on the physical earthly plane.

There are two key types of grounding you can do:

i) Physical grounding – try sitting in a chair with your feet flat on the floor, sitting cross-legged on the floor, or lying on the ground.
ii) Mental grounding – imagine golden roots growing out of the soles of your feet, connecting you to the magical earth beneath you, burying deeper and deeper until these roots reach the centre of the earth and wrap around the black obsidian crystal ball at the centre of the planet, grounding you to the earth.

If you cannot physically touch the earth with your feet, just place your feet flat on the floor of the place where you are sitting. For instance, I regularly meditate when I'm in an aeroplane or a car. Mental grounding will keep you rooted, enabling you to draw those messages clearly through into the earthly plane.

If, when you come out of a meditation, you feel a little lightheaded, just stomp your feet on the ground, clap your hands or eat some food. These 'earthly' actions, including the intention of being grounded, bring you fully into your body.

Protection is important because it sets the intention for the visualisation. I only ever choose to access my 'best and highest guidance'. This means I request to receive the most appropriate guidance from wise beings of pure love and light.

These beings could be Source, angels or beings as energetically well-intentioned and wise as angels. By asking for protection in the visualisation, we insulate our auras from everything but the angels or similarly pure beings and then we are 100% protected.

A quick thirty-second grounding and protection ritual is really useful to perform every morning or at any point during the day. Throughout the day, we are unknowingly bombarded by negative energy from everyday living - transport, crowds, demands, toxins and so on. Asking for protection provides an additional layer of protection against everyday life. I usually ask Archangel Michael for protection because he specialises in this.

An example of a request for protection would be the following:

> *Archangel Michael, please protect me with your blue cloak of protection. Please place it on my shoulders, zip it up from beneath my feet to beneath my chin, and pull the hood over my head so I am completely protected. Please then surround me with your angels of protection.*

When you make this request, pay attention to how you feel at an energetic level. Feel Archangel Michael placing his cloak on your shoulders, be aware of how safe you feel when he zips it up from beneath your feet to beneath your chin, and be aware of the hood covering your head.

You might not be able to feel this right away - and that's okay. As you work through the exercises in this book, take time to grow this sixth sense - your intuitive, energetic 'power'.

A Word on Unwanted Spirit Guests

In my experience, if we set the intention to connect only with angels or beings of pure love, we will connect only with angels or beings of pure love in our visualisations.

I personally choose to access only the highest and purest beings. I don't channel spirits that have passed over, as some mediums do. I will sometimes connect with my loved ones who have passed over, or to the loved ones of other people close to me. Sometimes a well-intentioned spirit will reach out to me to pass on a message. But I always foreground it with the intention that I will receive a message only if it is for 'my best and highest good'.

I've met some people who are scared of meditation because they feel it will expose them to unwanted spirits. However, rest assured that if you have a clear intention to access only beings of pure love, and if you avoid mind-altering drugs, you are not at risk.

Getting the Purest Message

I believe strongly that to access your highest guidance, you have to prepare your mind for purity and love. Think of it as physical purity and mental purity. We can ask for angelic protection or help at any time, day or night, whatever state we are in. But to receive the highest guidance, 'messages' from the angelic kingdom that we should trust, I believe it is important not to be under the influence of narcotics, including alcohol, marijuana, or any other drugs that affect our minds.

One famous angel author said in one of her books that even chocolate reduced her ability to connect with the angels. Fortunately, chocolate doesn't affect my ability to connect with the angels; but if you are finding it a little difficult to connect, look at your diet and what you're taking in.

Are you smoking, consuming a lot of meat or junk food, or trying to meditate in a very noisy place? Experiment with different places and variations in your normal lifestyle and see if that helps. Also remember that, like riding a bike, with a little bit of practice it will soon come naturally, and then you'll be able to connect with your angels at ease.

To prepare our minds to receive the highest guidance, notice that visualisations often start with a focus on breathing slowly and evenly, and imagining white light or healing energy flowing through us. This directs the body towards a calmer state of being, helping the mind let go of the stresses of the day.

Box 1: Dos and Don'ts of connecting with your angels in visualisation	
Do	Don't
• Sit with your legs slightly apart and your feet flat on the floor, or sit cross-legged, or lie on the floor • Close your eyes • Relax your shoulders • Become aware of your breathing • Breathe deeply and evenly (breathing is very important, as it calms the heart and tells the mind it can be calm) • Imagine golden roots burying out of the soles of your feet into the earth • Ask God, Archangel Michael, Jesus, the Prophet Mohammed or whichever wise being you resonate with for protection • Set your intention to invite only beings that have pure love for you • Experiment with different diets and places to meditate in, if you're finding connection difficult	• Drink alcohol or take other mind-influencing drugs the same day / day before you meditate • Smoke whilst meditating • Slouch when meditating • Cross your legs or your arms in meditation As a rule, beings of the highest love and light don't like drugs.

Chapter 3

THE EMOTIONAL ROLLERCOASTER

Birthing and raising a disabled child can be an emotional rollercoaster. The Kübler-Ross Curve depicted in Figure 1 was first introduced by Swiss-American psychiatrist Elisabeth Kübler-Ross in her 1969 book *On Death and Dying*, and was inspired by her work with terminally ill patients.[1] It has since been used in many different contexts of personal loss, including bereavement, job loss, divorce and trauma. It is equally relevant to the birth of a disabled child. It describes the series of emotions a person tends to pass through when faced with dramatic change. After the initial shock, denial gives way to anger and resistance, followed by depression and the lowest point of emotion. After that, things are predicted to get better: there is acceptance, enthusiasm and hope - and, eventually, commitment to a future path.

Emotional Response to Change

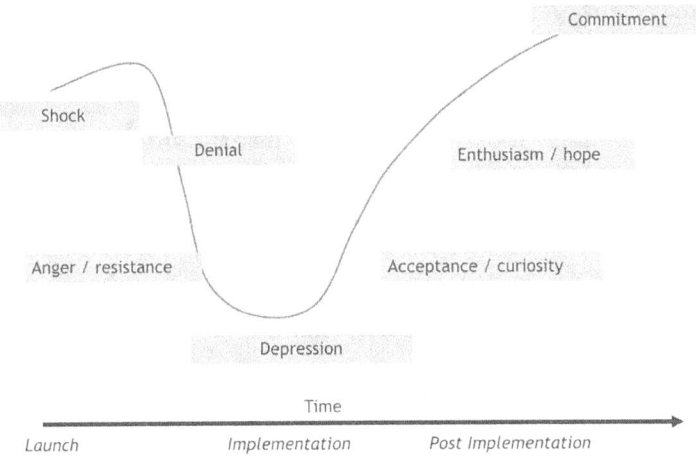

Figure 1: Single End-point Kübler-Ross Emotional Curve

However, since this initial methodology was first presented, Kübler-Ross and others have explained that emotions are not experienced in a linear procession and can sometimes be experienced in parallel or complex patterns. A more recent interpretation of the Curve describes the possibility of two end-states (see Figure 2). In one end state, a person undergoes a catharsis (the process of releasing, thereby experiencing relief from extreme and repressed emotions). Over time, the person accepts the end state and has a positive quality of life. In the other end state, rather than dealing with the trauma, the person falls into depression, resulting in a negative quality of life and the potential for crisis.

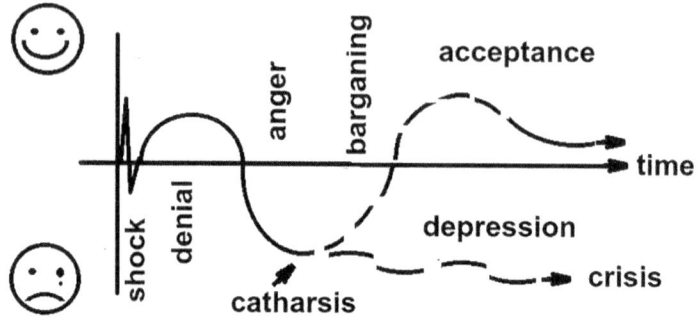

Figure 2 Two End-Point Kübler-Ross Emotional Curve

Ref: developed for Jobcentre Plus by Eos, Created: 19 November 2017

In my experience, having a disabled child is not a linear progression from catharsis through to acceptance or depression. It is not a one-off event that you either overcome or are compromised by. Saafi has had multiple health 'shocks' since his birth. He has been in hospital thrice with pneumonia, twice with infection, and had extended periods of illness requiring intensive efforts to stop him deteriorating further. On one occasion, he could barely sleep for six weeks because of discomfort. After tests, it seems he had developed a form of epilepsy, perhaps brought on by lung complications. With each 'shock' that could be fatal, I am plunged again into mental and sometimes physical exhaustion and worry, and a need to draw on the tools and resources in this book to clamber back out into thriving once more.

As our children get older they may develop different health challenges, sometimes greater than before. These can throw us back onto the emotional rollercoaster.

Therefore, it's important to be aware of the dynamic nature of disability and the need to be ever-vigilant about our own mental and physical health. The exercises and information in this book are geared towards recognizing this dynamic nature and can be repeated over the years to maintain resilience.

The aim of this book is to help you - through understanding the spiritual aspects of disability, combined with spiritual practice and practical tips - to realise the gift of our disabled children and ensure we end up in the positive end-state of acceptance in order to achieve our life purpose and full potential.

Shock and Denial

From the time of Saafi's birth, to the initial shock of him almost dying and finally the discovery of his prognosis of severe brain damage, I went through an extended period of denial. I clung to the seemingly limitless library of literature relating to plasticity in a baby's brain and the importance of stimulating babies in the first six months to three years. His father and I did everything we could to help Saafi's physical progress. He hadn't managed to latch onto my breast in hospital or upon our return home, so I expressed breast milk, as I wanted to ensure he had the best nutrition for his brain.

I had to teach him to drink from a cup, to be able to leave the hospital. I then spent three months painstakingly feeding him through tiny tubes on my finger, to try to teach him to suck. A single feeding sometimes took 1.5 hours. In the first year I also tried to get in as much 'kangaroo' time as I could, as I'd been advised skin-to-skin contact is important for mother-child bonding. So my day was a regimen of express for 30 minutes, feed for one hour, kangaroo or do other stuff for 1.5 hours. I maintained this demanding routine day and night. It was during this time that I read - mostly in the early hours of the morning - a tome called *The State of Africa*. Fascinating though it was, I don't think I'd ever have got through it if I hadn't had all those additional hours to myself when I normally would have been sleeping.

My mum says I was born 'sunshine and showers' but I've taught myself the habit of positive thinking, so most of the time now I'm *sunshine*. Therefore, I wouldn't accept the neurologist's prognosis. This denial is partly in my character, but when I came across the Kübler-Ross diagram I learned that it is a standard response to trauma or shock.

Perhaps this is a natural way for the mind to cope with the unexpected. When I think back on this time, which lasted until Saafi was about three years old, it was both a nightmare of fear and an extended period of hope. In some ways, it seemed to be happening to someone else. It was so far outside my frame of reference and what I'd ever predicted my life would entail. It was also a period of trying everything we could.

I was running on survival mode, taking one day at a time. When Saafi finally started making noises, he cried much of the time for the first 1.5 years, which is tough for any parent. In the South African private health system, unlike in the UK where I am from, there isn't a central coordinated approach to an individual's healthcare. You are the client, so you go and ask for service. It was easy to feel left on our own, as parents.

We were and are inordinately lucky to have a supportive therapy school close to us, which has been a rock of support. We also have an excellent paediatrician to support us, but those first few years still felt like we were searching in the dark. We tried every alternative treatment we could think of: Saafi was on charcoal and energy healing, and then we tried the Anat Baniel Method, as well as more conventional physiotherapy, occupational therapy and speech therapy. Saafi's father also created crawling and walking aids, and contraptions to help him practise reaching, and we both gave him a lot of physical stimulation.

Amidst this, I had a beautiful older son to look after. I had also left my permanent UK-Aid diplomatic job a year earlier so the family could stay in South Africa and enable my South African husband, who was near retirement, to realise his full pension. During pregnancy, I had taken on a new consultancy position that didn't come with maternity leave. So, once Saafi turned four months, I started working from home two days a week. To make up for these two days, I was up and down to my office five days in the week.

The bits of time I could work were carved out of feeding, expressing and childcare time. My husband was very supportive in terms of practical things like getting jars for the vast quantities of milk I was stockpiling and regularly taking Saafi to his therapy centre, but he was also going through his own emotional journey.

Anger Towards Myself

I directed my anger mostly towards myself, combined with a large sack-load of guilt. I went over and over in my mind what I could have done differently during my pregnancy or the birth.

During my pregnancy I had felt great. I'd had so much energy - but I had taken a new job and experienced extreme stress at work, with a boss who had anger management problems. When I came home, I was faced with a husband who also had anger problems. After one particularly bad week of my being bullied at work, Saafi, in the womb, told me he was damaged. A few weeks after, I went in for my regular scan and Saafi showed a drop in estimated weight from average to the lowest percentile. Doctors were worried he might not be receiving enough oxygen or nutrition. Subsequent tests couldn't substantiate this and it was too early to take Saafi out of the womb, as he wouldn't have survived. So, I continued working, now based from home rather than in the office.

Being psychic is a gift, but it's also not always straightforward. In 2011, when I started receiving direct communication from Source, I committed to following my Guidance 100%. It was around the sixteen-week marker that I was offered another job. I initially turned it down. My Guidance said: don't do it. But the offer on the table seemed so right. The company partner trying to recruit me knew I was pregnant and emphasized the child-friendly nature of the company, I would be able to home work, I could initially come back to work for just three days a week, and they would remunerate me well. In contrast, my current employer thought pregnancy was a distraction and told me I'd be useless when I returned to work with a fudge brain; the commute was long and the contract duration unclear. I knew my husband felt the job being offered was preferable.

I negotiated hard with my Guidance. The offer on the table seemed so much more compatible with a young family than my current role. Source just kept repeating, 'It's not going to happen. You can go for it, but it will be stressful'. Torn in two, I decided to take up the new offer. What happened then I have never otherwise experienced in my career. Essentially, the new job pivoted around a partnership between two firms. Whilst my firm had the expertise, the other firm had signed the contract and I got caught up in internecine firm warfare – with the contracted firm wanting me replaced by their own person. The job never happened but the process, as my Guidance had predicted, proved extremely stressful.

In trying to understand where my fault lay in Saafi's outcome, I delved into every detail of this difficult set of circumstances.

Should I have left my first job earlier and avoided the stress? But then, people have healthy babies in warzones or as refugees, and most women work when they're pregnant, these days.

Should I have followed my Guidance and not taken the second job? But I thought I was doing the best thing for my family.

Should I have taken better nutritional supplements?

I even questioned my water birth – should I have had a caesarean like most private patients in South African hospitals (94%!)? Should I have insisted on having a doctor on-site, even though the midwife was the most experienced in Pretoria and we were birthing in an integrated annex at the hospital, so medical help was there if anything went wrong? My gynaecologist had also given me a clean bill of health, a seal of approval to have a natural birth.

With the medical evidence currently available, it seems we will never know for certain the 'earthly cause'. But when Saafi was born, the midwife discovered the placenta was very calcified, indicating an old placenta, even though Saafi was two weeks early. Also, the umbilical cord wasn't deeply embedded in the placenta. This, combined with Saafi's relatively low birthweight, suggests his growth in the womb was constrained and thus the most likely contributor to his condition. However, why the placenta became like this, we will never know.

Anger from a Mate

As the years progressed, I began to experience increasingly intense animosity from my husband. Since we'd married, he'd commonly exhibited episodes of anger and emotional withdrawal, if I did something that displeased him. As it became clearer Saafi was not improving, these episodes seemed to become longer and more intense. Even when a car drove into the back of me, leaving me shaken, he merely said, 'So what?'

He found it extremely difficult that I was working, and my work often took me away from home for five days per month and occasionally longer. But the necessity of earning a double income was clear, as Saafi's health was compromised and medical research said that 60% of children with severe cerebral palsy die by the age of 20; 40% lived well past that. We had to plan and save for Saafi's maintenance and well-being long after his parents had stopped earning or passed away. There were also other benefits to my job, including medical insurance and home working. At all other times than when I was travelling, I was in the house full-time. This meant that although Saafi had a care-giver, I could supervise her at all times.

During the times I was away for work, the burden fell on my husband, supported by a nanny. On several occasions when the nanny was sick, he had to look after the boys on his own. This was tough on him.

I realised the work was also an outlet for me, a place where I could forget the daily worries; but in hindsight, I also realize it was an energizer. I received affirmation from work; I was praised and thanked. In the role of mother,

I felt out of control of the situation and I wasn't finding affirmation of my efforts, in the household. Work was a constant, an anchor.

Several times my husband said it was my fault Saafi had cerebral palsy. He never clarified what he thought I'd done, but this compounded my own guilt that I should have done something, even though intellectually, medically and spiritually I knew I was not to blame.

It is very common for mothers to blame themselves for compromised health or disability in their children. Given that we've carried the child in our womb, we feel it's our job to protect the unborn baby, so that in some way we must be responsible when something happens to them. Sadly, it is also very common for fathers to blame the mothers. When a person hurts, they sometimes look for the nearest person to blame and one of the obvious candidates is the mother – or, sometimes, other children. One of the worst names he called me was a 'shit mother'. It attacked one of the most sacred parts of myself.

Those days were in many ways the worst. I can remember times when my older boy, in tears, asked, 'Why is Daddy shouting at you?' and then started to intervene and stand up for me. At the time, he was only seven.

Control

I have always been committed to self-exploration in my adult life. I've trained in Kahuna massage, which is a deep spiritual Hawaiian massage that teaches you about body reading and releasing trapped emotions from your body, from this and previous lives. I've trained in kinesiology, a powerful way to release blockages and negative patterns from this life and ancestral / past lives. I've read and meditated extensively, with the aim of becoming a better person. I've also undertaken intensive periods of therapy with personal psychologists and marriage counsellors. I believe that in the end, there is only one person in the room anyway: we have to work on our own stuff before we're ready to have healthy relationships with others.

It was only when Saafi was about two that I felt ready to discuss the subject of his disability with my psychologist. Until then, I hadn't seen any need. I think this was part of the denial. I hadn't wanted to join any parent support groups either. When I eventually discussed the subject of Saafi and the journey I had gone through, one interesting thing the therapist suggested was that my dedication to expressing milk enabled me to exert control in my life when other parts of my life were out of control.

The quantity of milk I expressed was impressive to pretty much any onlooker. I first filled one upright freezer, and then my husband bought me another trunk freezer, which I also filled. I knew the essential importance of breast milk to a baby – but more particularly, breast milk is excellent for the brain, and I desperately wanted to do anything I could for Saafi's brain. I thought if I had an extra year's supply of milk after I stopped expressing at one or so years, then he would have good brain juice for over two years, and that could only be a good thing.

Expressing was a commitment. I hired an industrial double-breast pump. I had a weird fetish-looking express bra, which really helped milk flow, as I could express without holding the milk bottles to my breast. Being so much more relaxed, the milk flowed more easily. I kept up the day-and-night ritual until Saafi was sixteen months old. Some days I pumped over one litre of milk. I kept all my daily quantities of expressed milk written neatly in a little notebook so I could compare the quantities expressed over time. It also caused both my husband and me anxiety, as our 'milk bank' was an invaluable treasure that couldn't be replaced. When we had one of the regular power cuts in the neighbourhood, we needed a generator to ensure the freezers could continue to keep the milk frozen.

The irony was that Saafi didn't like the frozen milk once defrosted. He refused it point blank. And I only tried it on him when I had stopped producing my own milk. Whilst some was fresh enough to give to the local milk bank to help premature babies, most had to be thrown out. It's strange to me that this rejection and waste of milk didn't faze me. I think in a way the milk had fulfilled its purpose. I had done everything I could to help Saafi to reach his full physical potential.

Fear and Anxiety

I have felt my fair share of fear and anxiety over Saafi's five years so far. For any loving parent, it is painful to see your child suffer. Saafi has been in hospital twice with pneumonia and had at least one period of extended illness where he seemed to be in severe pain – on one occasion, this went on for over one month and he was diagnosed with epilepsy. When your child can't talk, it adds an additional layer of frustration and fear, as you don't know exactly what they are feeling or where they are hurting. We are also not clear how much Saafi understands, although we work on the assumption that he is cognitively 100% sharp and it is just his physical condition that is challenged. All the standard IQ tests are based on physical interaction and developmental milestones. When a child can't sit, control his arms, hands, legs, tongue or head, it makes it impossible for them to demonstrate their intellectual ability.

The relatively frequent spells of life-threatening chest infections and epilepsy, along with the medical prognosis that six out of ten children with level-five cerebral palsy do not reach the age of twenty, create a situation of either acute fear (when you're in the midst of a medical episode) or background fear (the knowledge that health and lungs are compromised).

However, there can also be other fear drivers – for instance, money. There is the need to manage health bills in the short term. Saafi needs 24-hour care and a range of therapy and additional interventions to maximise his quality of life.

As mentioned, there is also the need to plan for Saafi's comfort and well-being throughout his life and in the event he outlives his parents. Whilst there is the risk of early mortality, there is also the hope of living a long life. With medical advances happening all the time, this is very much a possibility.

There are anxieties about the future. As a child grows, they become heavier and simple things like bathing and going out require special aids and planning. Depending on where you live in the world, the level of healthcare and what is publicly available or available at your own cost is radically different.

THE SPIRITUAL SIDE OF DISABILITY

Photo 3a and 3b: Saafi's Breast Milk Bank

Depression and Feeling Overwhelmed

Over the years, I've learnt the habit of happiness. Most days I don't drop below a 7 out of 10 on the happiness scale, come rain or shine, and I think this has really helped my levels of resilience. This book shares some of the exercises and practices I've done to develop this positivity and resilience. Fortunately I have never felt depressed, perhaps in large part due to the resources I draw on and outline in this book. But at times I have felt overwhelmed and extremely tearful.

One of the crisis points for me was when my husband, our two children and I were on holiday in my birth village and staying in a little property I own there, opposite my parents and the house where I was born. My father called me to a family meeting at their house. Both he and my mum were present. My dad – who runs children's social services in the area where we are from – said that if we lived in the UK, he would have my children taken away from me because of the behaviour he'd witnessed from the children's father towards them and me. I was shocked and devastated. I thought one married for life, come thick or thin, and the nuclear family was the best thing for the children. However, I had witnessed my older son copying my husband's behaviour. Aged just seven, he had started shouting at me frequently.

On one occasion I challenged him and asked, 'Why are you shouting at me?'

'Because you like it', he said.

Why would you think I like it?' I asked.

'Because Daddy shouts at you all the time and you married him, so you must like it', he replied.

These two events – my father's wake-up call and my son telling me I liked being shouted at – were pivotal. They may have been low points, but they made it clear to me that things had to change. I couldn't stay and manage my husband's depression and mood swings *and* be the mum I needed to be for my two beautiful boys. I needed to leave, for my own health and that of my children. But it took me a further two years – amid threats that I'd lose my children, navigating an unfamiliar legal system where the mother doesn't automatically get custody of the children, undergoing further marriage counselling and planning a smooth separation for the children – to get to a point where a positive separation was possible.

When I thought I was on the home run, I was put under another extreme test. The perfect storm came along, where I felt assaulted on all sides. I'd moved out, had bought my own beautiful home just around the corner from my ex, to ease the transition for the children. Tariq had helped me choose it and here the children were really happy. I'd established a balanced, working relationship with the children moving between me and their father.

But life wasn't smooth. I was facing a hostile divorce, with my ex accusing me of negligence towards Saafi (without any evidence of what I'd supposedly done), suing me for full custody of the children and controlling a significant amount of our joint wealth – money I'd invested with him 50:50 from my own salary. Saafi had gone through a severe health crisis for an extended period of about six weeks where during many nights he couldn't sleep, was constantly whimpering and was rigid like a board. This was when he was diagnosed with epilepsy. I was diagnosed with medical exhaustion brought on by years of chronic stress stemming from emotional abuse and managing Saafi's condition (from an emotional perspective, largely on my own).

What finally pushed me to my limits was that the job that had been my anchor, my source of affirmation and financial security, unexpectedly came to an end with no redundancy pay, as I was employed as a consultant. My savings only covered three months' living expenses and my husband was only intermittently contributing to the boys' private medical, dental, therapy and schooling costs.

The financial insecurity I felt in having to manage two mortgages (a small property in the UK and the property I'd bought upon leaving my husband's house) – and being 'trapped' in South Africa because my husband refused to allow the children to leave – meant I couldn't take up an opportunity my employer offered me back in the UK.

I felt bombarded from all quarters. I had numerous dreams where a tsunami was raging towards me. I also had dreams about being tracked by a serial killer. What was I going to do?

Acceptance and Finding the Platinum Lining

'It never helps to feel sorry for yourself'. This was a piece of advice my strong, stoic, loving mother gave me when I was a child. It's something I try to embrace as an adult. I think it's fine to feel sorry for yourself for a short while, but it doesn't help the situation. What helps is to get practical – get practical and get spiritual.

I write lots of lists. I love lists – lists of actions that need to be taken, and relevant dates attached to each action. This helps me organise my thoughts. But to know what lists to write, it's essential to first know what you're aiming to achieve.

For many years I've meditated on what my ideal life would look like and then turned this vision into time-bound goals of where I want to be and by when. During this 'tough' period I found an awesome 'planner' that broke years, months, weeks and days down into 'goals'. This was perfect for me. I used this to identify where I wanted to get to and by when, combined with visioning and discussion with my Guidance.

For me, I felt strongly that the Universe, by pulling my job from under my feet and essentially forcing me to have some time *not working*, was giving me the space to do what I knew I was meant to do: write this book. It's so easy to make excuses, e.g. *I have no time; I'm too busy to write, what with work and children.* I felt deeply that if I didn't address the request my Guidance was making of me, to write this book, I would be faced with even harder lessons until I woke up and listened.

I also felt my Guidance was giving me a clear, insightful lesson that to be spiritual does not mean you shun money. To the contrary, to be spiritual your material needs should be taken care of. Living in fervent fear of not being able to pay your child's therapy bills, the medical insurance or the mortgage for your house does not create the mental mindset to be 'spiritual' and calm. Money is absolutely not the *be all and end all*, but it plays its part.

It is also vital to love yourself enough to accept that you deserve security and comfort. That doesn't mean you should allow yourself to get caught up in materialistic competition; it does mean accepting you are worthy of feeling safe and secure, and enjoying the flow of abundance that can come to us.

I recognise that a repeating pattern in my life is fear of losing my house. When I was a child, one of my most traumatic memories is when my grandfather died and the house I was initially raised in with my mum and grandparents was going to be sold. This home was where I had my happiest memories. Later in life, this situation was repeated several times. One of the lessons you find you must learn may be that it is okay to let go: something better (a better house, for instance) will come in its place. Another lesson may be to accept you are worthy of security and easily affording the house you want.

Through my Guidance and envisioning, this is the 'to do' list I last compiled for my own life:

- Fulfil my spiritual calling – write this book, publish my other spiritual books, get this message out there.
- Have a job that I love, that provides me with financial security and abundance, where I perform brilliantly, I am appreciated, and I can help the world.
- Have a smooth, swift, fair divorce and achieve at least joint access to my children – ideally, gain primary custody of them, where I am free to take

them to see my parents and family and even live overseas with them.
- Be healthy and empowered – realise my Inner Goddess, as I term it – ensure my health (including hair, teeth, nails, skin, physical fitness and strength) are honoured, and continue to learn new skills that will empower me and allow me to regain my zest for life.

With this list ever in mind, I used the opportunity to see what lessons I could learn. I went deep into myself and challenged buried belief systems. The following came up for me:

- Money – I still had deep-seated resistance when it came to feeling I deserved financial security. It has been neurologically proven that we hold several generations of our ancestors' belief systems in our brains. We can re-programme our brains, but it takes systematic attention of at least 21 days.[1] So, I found a great book that addressed this by a world-famous hypnotist, including audio I could listen to every day to 're-programme' my mind. I also repeated some self-tailored affirmations to myself each morning and evening.
- Self-worth – my husband had consistently called me a variety of hurtful names, including 'shit mother', 'financially irresponsible', 'materialistic', 'selfish', 'self-centred', 'idiot', 'useless', 'shit wife', and so on. I had also absorbed the names and insults that my boss with the anger management problem had levelled at me: 'colonial

---

[1] Dr Caroline Leaf, 'Switch on Your Brain', 2013, Baker Books.

racist', 'unlikeable', 'naïve', 'you know nothing', 'stupid'. I 'went into' each of these insults, assessed the truth and formed my own views. For the custody case, I had to provide a physical file counteracting my husband's accusations of me, to demonstrate my ability as a mother and my right to look after my children. Building a factual case was a strongly empowering process for me, as it helped me see that I was the polar opposite of the woman he had tried to make me believe I was.

I matched delving deep spiritually with clear, focused action. We are physical beings and I don't believe most of us can reach our highest potential by simply sitting on a mat and meditating. If our health is suffering, we need to address the root cause, which usually includes doing exercise and eating healthily, as well as reducing our stressors. If we don't have a job, we need to put ourselves out there and find one – apply, circulate our CV, tell people we are looking and available. Getting practical is part of our spiritual journey. We need to push ourselves out of our comfort zones and take some risks.

When I was a young girl, my grandmother, whom I was very close to, would sometimes show me an heirloom she had gifted me in her will. It was enclosed in a petite tan leather case, kept in a satin bag full of white embroidered handkerchiefs, hidden in her dresser drawer. The heirloom was a diamond-and-platinum necklace, very old and beautiful. She would tell me how platinum is even more valuable than gold. So when I think of the most precious material gift we can be given, I think of platinum. And when I think of finding the silver linings in situations, I don't stop at silver; I look for platinum linings. These are the deepest, most powerful linings of those storm clouds that sometimes shake our world.

As I write this with much trust, faith, positive thinking, meditation and action, things have turned yet another corner – this time, a positive one. I have a splendid new job, Saafi is well, there is a date for the divorce hearing (albeit over a year from now) and my children are extremely happy. I am also listening to my Guidance and moving forward with what I know I must do: write this book and share my experience.

With all these challenges, I have never felt depressed or without hope. These are challenges given to us to make us the most spiritually evolved we can be by learning soul lessons. I am excited to share the tools that have helped me, and to help you communicate directly with the celestial kingdom and the friends, mentors and power sources waiting for you to make contact.

Chapter 4
SOUL CONTRACTS & OUR PURPOSE AS HUMANS ON EARTH

Earth is a training ground. It's one of the most difficult and popular in the spirit plane. We don't always get what we want; we have to *work* at our own happiness.

There are a number of influential books that provide evidence of the life between lives, i.e. the place where souls go between incarnations on Earth. On my website (details at the end of this book), I list some that I have found particularly compelling. In this spirit domain, as souls, we have perfect memory and understanding. We know our connection to God and we understand the tests we need to endure and pass in the physical plane – on Earth – to progress with our spiritual ascension (becoming an enlightened being).

When we have completed and passed all tests on Earth, and we are wise enough to graduate, we become Ascended Masters – wise and pure beings who have experienced a human evolution (as opposed to an angelic evolution, for instance).

Souls come back and back to Earth in different incarnations until they graduate. Before a soul incarnates, it discusses with its spirit guide (often its Guardian Angel) the lessons it still needs to learn and agrees to the 'vessel' (the body) it will take on in the next lifetime. There any many lessons created by the body we take on, so the vessel is an important choice.

When a soul chooses its body, it chooses its gender, race, physical features and physical ability or disability.

Entering a body as a child with a severe disability or debilitating disease is reserved for more advanced souls – souls that have already incarnated many times and learned many lessons.

Soul Contracts

Before a soul incarnates, it also discusses the different major soul contracts it will have with significant humans in the next lifetime. This includes agreeing to its parents, children, close friends, major influencers or challengers in life. If you've ever come across someone you've found particularly challenging in your life, this is likely to emanate from a soul contract with that person. It may be that you are repaying karma (energetic debt) with a soul. It may be that you chose the same souls to contract with in multiple lives. This is sometimes called your soul family, and the different members of the family may come back in different family roles, e.g. father in one life, child in another.

Even people who are really horrible to you may, at the soul level, be in your soul family, as their soul may have agreed with your soul, before incarnation, to teach you a certain lesson. As an example, perhaps you have a father who abandoned you during childhood. He may actually be teaching you the lesson of unconditional love for yourself, by forcing you to find a way to love yourself despite being made to feel worthless.

Therefore, it is important to look for the lessons in everything. It shouldn't excuse the poor behaviour of others – but understanding the soul level contract can help release feelings of anger and resentment and aid in forgiveness. In one powerful regression I did on forgiveness, I asked for an explanation of the seemingly poor treatment directed towards me by a person in this lifetime. I was shocked to regress to a previous life about eight hundred years ago, which I was told was the last incarnation we had lived together.

In that life, this person was my father and I his son. I remember the act of killing him out of greed. I was told that, at the soul level, in this life I was repaying a karmic debt to him for this wrong I had done him many lifetimes ago. Rather than him wronging me in this lifetime, he was helping me balance my karma, an essential part of our personal ascension (becoming an enlightened being).

Exercise: Finding Patterns in Your Life

Write a five-minute history of your personal life, noting the most significant events since your birth.

Under each event, note the emotion you associate with it. Then, read through your notes.

Can you see any patterns repeated in this storyline? Are there events or types of experience that occur more than once? Are there any repeated emotions, such as fear, guilt, rejection, abandonment, joy, love, wonder?

> Becoming aware of underlying patterns and emotions is part of the healing journey and will lay the foundation for the visualisations you will undertake in the rest of this book.

Karma

Before they enter Earth in their first incarnation, a blueprint is agreed for the soul, with the soul's Guardian Angel. The blueprint states the ultimate potential of the soul and the key lessons that need to be mastered before Ascension can take place. Ascension is where the sixth dimension is attained and the soul can graduate from the school of Earth, stop reincarnating, and continue learning in the celestial realms or other training grounds. Once on Earth, souls re-incarnate again and again, until the lessons are completed.

When a person dies, their soul must stand before the Karmic Board, a committee of Ascended Masters and cosmic beings. Here they will be assessed, and their karma will be weighed up (their good deeds against their bad deeds) and recorded in the Akashic Records. This is most likely where the idea of Judgement Day came from. However, the assessment is done within the context of pure love and without judgement.

The next step is for the soul, their Guardian Angel and the Karmic Board to decide the key lessons for the next incarnation and identify the soul contracts that need to be made. By understanding these soul contracts and the karma on which they are based, the relationships you find most challenging can be recognised as enabling you to progress along your best and highest path. The people you find most difficult or who hurt you the most become your *best teachers*. In this way, you can honour them at a soul level with unconditional love, and release hurts and resentments.

Unconditional love and forgiveness are very closely linked. For if you love unconditionally, seeing past people's exterior imperfections to their soul – along with soul contracts – forgiveness will flow.

Accepting and Letting Go

A central part of attaining the happy state of parenting a disabled child, rather than going into depression and crisis mode, is to acknowledge the feelings we feel and let them go. We mustn't feel guilty about experiencing negative emotions. It is part of our spiritual journey to work through these 'tests'. Negative emotions stem from our 'ego', which separates us from our soul level knowledge. The visualisations in this section help you let go of these emotions, with the help of the angels and particular celestial beings. You can repeat them whenever it feels necessary. Keep a record of what you experience in these visualisations, in your notebook.

A Word on Death

For many people, death is a frightening thought. Even when we have religious beliefs that tell of an afterlife, this doesn't always comfort people. Some religious approaches instil a sense of fear (think of Judgement Day). Others may believe there probably is something coming after death, but they are unsure what it is. One of the challenges has been that religion doesn't require proof, just 'faith'.

When we plan to have children, our expectation or hope is that they will outlive us. However, it is a relatively recent phenomenon, and one characterised more by the so-called 'developed' world, that our children will almost certainly outlive us. In many countries around the world, infant mortality remains tragically high.

Worldwide, in the year 2000 54 infants out of 1,000 died before one year of age. In 2016 it was estimated to be 31 infants per 1,000 births. Notably, in 2017 Afghanistan had 110.6 infant deaths per 1,000 live births and in Somalia, the next-worst, there were 94.8 infant deaths per 1,000 live births. By contrast, the lowest death rates (below 5 deaths per 1,000 live births) were in Europe, Hong Kong, South Korea, North America, et al. Monaco had the fewest deaths per 1,000 live births in 2017 at just 1.8, closely followed by Japan at 2.

When we have a disabled child, depending on the type of disability, early death is a possibility. For any parent in this situation, I strongly recommend you read into techniques to discuss mortality with both your disabled child and their siblings, but also to come to terms with it yourself. Several times strangers have approached me and told me with a warm smile that they had a brother, cousin or nephew just like my son who lived almost until they were 20. I know they are just trying to connect with me, but it does amaze me how people think it is acceptable to suggest to a stranger that their son is likely to die before age 20.

I have researched the life expectancy of my son and consulted with experts, and this has been empowering. As parents, we must *plan for the long term but live in the now* to ensure we appreciate every minute we have with our child, in case he does decide to pass over from us early. I believe Saafi will be with us as long as his soul wants to be, and I am committed to giving his life meaning and joy and filling it with love and adventure for the time he is with us.

From a spiritual viewpoint, I understand death to be a wonderful homecoming. I have researched into proof of the afterlife and it has confirmed what my Guidance has described to me. When you die, you are met by your Guardian Angel, who chaperones you across the bridge between the earthly plane and spiritual plane. There, you are met by people from all your past lives, the souls of loved ones you remember now that the Veil of Amnesia has been lifted. There is a joyous party, and then you go into a sort of debriefing, where your spirit plane mentor takes you through the life you have just finished and the decisions you made. They discuss with you the lessons you were meant to learn from the soul contracts agreed before that incarnation, and what lessons you still need to learn. Most of us then identify with our mentors the lessons needed to be tested in the next incarnation on Earth. If we have done well and learnt our lessons well enough, we can choose not to incarnate on Earth again but to continue our training in the spirit plane.

Two books I would highly recommend in terms of the proof of the afterlife are *Proof of Heaven* by Eben Alexander and *Destiny of Souls* by Michael Newton. Eben Alexander is a neurosurgeon who went into a coma, became clinically brain dead, went to Heaven and then returned fully recovered. Because of his training, he knew the only scientific explanation for his experience was that he had actually gone to Heaven. It is a fascinating read.

Michael Newton is a psychologist who accidentally regressed a patient to the life between lives. He then purposefully took his other patients into the life between earthly lives and found that they all experienced the same thing when they died: a joyous homecoming with spirit loved ones. Both these books are wonderfully affirming about what awaits us.

Whilst there is no replacement for our loved ones when they pass over to the other side, I find it is some consolation that they will go to somewhere special. I have connected psychically with my loved ones after they have passed over, and whilst there is sometimes a period of confusion as they find their feet, so to speak, after a short time in the spirit world (what we might call Heaven) they are always incredibly happy and full of joy. It is also a comfort to know that we will see our loved ones again when we pass over.

Finding Your Soul Purpose

I don't know about you, but going through what I have with Saafi has taught me so many lessons about myself and about life. I've experienced so many intense emotions and I am now quite a different being than the one before Saafi came along. In the next chapters, we'll explore this further, as well as ways to handle some of the emotional challenges of the journey.

But first, try the powerful visualisations that follow, to give you insight into the soul contract you have with your disabled child. You can also use the same visualisation with other significant people in your life.

Remember to write down your thoughts in a journal or notebook, as you progress through this book.

This section aims to provide different ways to get to understand your soul contract with your child and also your life's highest purpose – namely, what is the highest contribution you can make to the world in this lifetime.

Visualisation to Understand the Soul Contracts with Your Disabled Children

Feel your feet firmly on the floor. Feel tiny golden roots leave the soles of your feet and burrow into the soil, grounding you to Mother Earth.

Ask Archangel Michael to protect you in a ball or shroud of his blue energy of protection.

Ask your Guardian Angel to wrap its wings around you, protecting you 100%.

You find yourself on a grassy meadow. The sun is warm but gentle, and butterflies flit across the colourful flowers around you.

To your left is a meandering river. As you watch, a golden barge threads its way along the river and stops beside you. Upon it is a shining figure.

The figure steps off the barge and you recognise it as your disabled child's highest self. Highest selves are our souls, all the wisest and purest parts of a person.

You greet your disabled child and (s)he comes to meet you. You feel their unconditional love for you. You feel their peace and joy.

Ask your disabled child what life lessons (s)he is helping you learn, as agreed in your soul contract – the contract both your souls agreed to before your child incarnated.

Listen to what (s)he has to say. Ask any questions you may have. When you have finished, thank your disabled child and send them unconditional love. Also receive the unconditional love they send to you.

(S)he now steps onto the golden barge and sails away.

When you are ready, become aware of your breathing. Rub your fingers with your thumbs and open your eyes. Write down the messages you received.

Don't judge what messages you receive in this visualisation. Just note down any messages. Also become aware of any ideas that come to you over the course of this book. You are developing your connection with the celestial kingdom and your deep intuition. It might not come immediately.

The soul contract may simply be for you to learn to love yourself and others unconditionally. It could be to lead you to open a school for disabled children, retrain in a therapy that can help your own and other children, or to rebalance karma by honouring this soul in this lifetime. If you receive a sensation but no words or messages, just write that down. There is no right or wrong in visualisations and there is no correct speed of aptitude!

✦ Visualisation: Understanding Your Life Purpose ✦

Ground and protect yourself, as described above.

Imagine you are standing in a beautiful meadow. To your right, a quiet river meanders. To your left is an inviting forest where you can hear waterfalls trickle and birds sing. The air is warm and subtly sweet with the scent of flower blossom. In front of you, in the distance, is an impressive white marble building with a turret and a large entrance. Two massive columns stand on either side of the entrance.

You move swiftly and soundlessly towards the Library of Life. You can choose to fly if you prefer, for you have this natural ability and golden wings that lift you with ease. As you near the Library you see a glowing turquoise light emanating from a majestic Archangel. This is Archangel Michael and he is waiting for you.

You land or stop easily beside Archangel Michael. He greets you by placing one hand on your forehead and another on your heart. He then tells you why you are here: 'This is the Library of Life and within it there is a volume of the highest potential for your own life. Find this book, open it and receive the messages you need to receive.'

'How will I know which book it is?' you ask.

'The book will call to you', he answers.

The high wooden door swings inward, inviting you to enter. You follow Archangel Michael inside. You are calm and excited to know your life's highest purpose. But how will the book call to you?

The air is cooler inside. There is no synthetic lighting in the voluminous Library; natural light streaks in from a glass turret way, way up above you. There are hundreds of floors. Maybe thousands.

'The Library contains books on the lives of all the humans who have ever lived', he tells you.

Your eyes graze across the different floors. The books are in shade, as the natural light only falls upon the centre of the room where you now stand. As you look upwards, your eyes are drawn to a pulsating golden light. This is the book of your life calling to you. It is many, many floors up.

Your wings are powerful and Archangel Michael is there to help you fly, if you need additional help.

You rise smoothly upwards. Your body feels weightless. You alight on the landing where your gleaming golden book is. You reach up for it and it seems to move into your hands of its own energy.

Archangel Michael waits as you place it on a podium. You open it fearlessly.

Inside the book are words, messages, images and impressions. Receive information about your life purpose now.

Archangel Michael helps you interpret what you have seen, heard and read. Ask him any questions you have. Seek the clarity you need at this time.

When you have spent the time you need in the Library, replace the book on the shelf and gently fly back down to ground level. Leave the Library and, after thanking Archangel Michael for his help, return to the room.

Write down every message you received.

Chapter 5

THE HEART OF WELL-BEING

Our well-being is comprised of different aspects within our life. Each aspect contributes to our happiness.

1) Spiritual and personal development: this is your spiritual aspirations and any self-development you want to do.
2) Family: this includes your children and any goals you have to support your children's health, education and well-being. It can also include your non-spousal family goals.
3) Love and partner: this relates to your romantic aspirations.
4) Leisure and self-nurturing: this relates to 'you' time. It could also include time with friends.
5) Career: this relates to your day-to-day job or your career aspirations.
6) Finances: this relates to your financial security aspirations.

7) Health: this relates to your physical and mental health and fitness.
8) Giving back: this relates to a way you can contribute to the world, your community or someone else. It could be giving to charity or contributing your time in some way; or it could relate to your career or spiritual work, if that is contributing to the world or other people's well-being.

Our minds respond positively to clear goals in these different aspects of our life. One thing you may notice is how many categories there are. Sometimes I see mums, especially, squash their lives into essentially two categories – family and career – or sometimes even into just one – family.

For me, to be at my best and most centred, I require balance; and whilst some of the above categories may take up more time than others, consider how each of these categories, if given attention, could enrich your life.

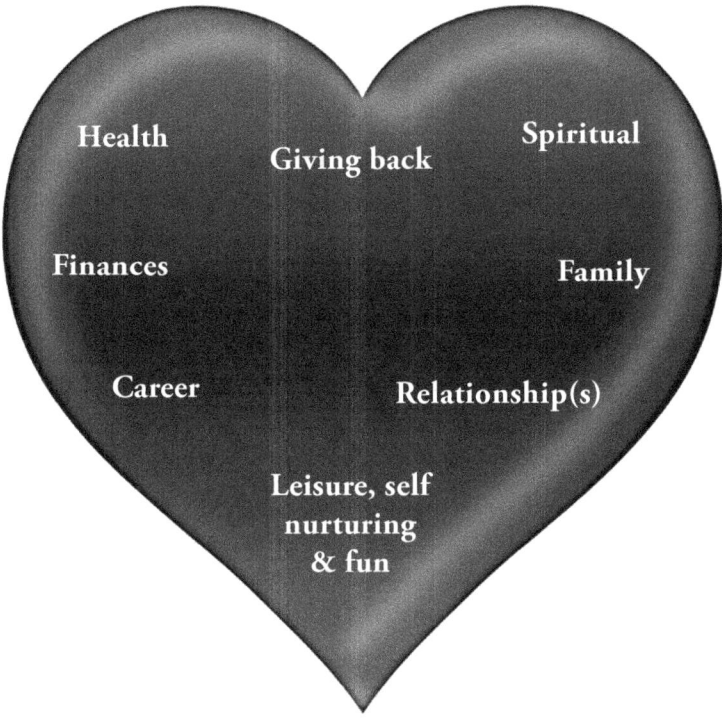

**Figure 3: The Heart of Emotional Wellbeing
- aspects of our life that need nurturing**

In this chapter, we will focus on spiritual and personal development, as well as nurturing – such an important topic. The most important thing you can do for your disabled child is protect your own health and happiness. I have seen many wonderful mothers who are martyrs to their children – they put the children before themselves, always. Often these mothers are shadows of what they could be.

I have seen many good mothers and fathers who beat themselves up about what happened, or how things 'should' have been different. I have seen other parents unable to talk about their experience, and I hear terrible stories about parents who are judged by their family, friends and community for seeking some leisure time and leaving their child with a caregiver, or going to work and not focusing exclusively on their child.

Spirituality and Personal Development

For me, my spiritual connection with Source, the Archangels and Ascended Masters has been a powerhouse of energy for me to draw on. Without my Guidance from Source, accessed through techniques introduced in this book, I wouldn't have excelled like I believe I have.

Finishing the exercises in this book could be an excellent one-year goal. A longer-term goal could be to connect on a regular basis with your Guardian Angel, or to make meditation a daily part of your practice. These are a few approaches you can consider:

- ✓ I undertake daily affirmations to project positive thinking into the day and to attract things I want into my life. Currently I affirm, 'Amazing things will happen to me today'. You never know what wonderful things are around the corner. I've been offered jobs on days that I say this. Think about what you want and find an affirmation that responds to it, e.g. 'An abundance of love/money/luck/wisdom is flowing into my life'.
- ✓ I talk to my highest guidance (usually Source, but it could be your Guardian Angel, or Jesus or Prophet Mohammed) when I need advice. I listen to what they have to say – either through channelling or by taking myself into a meditation.

- ✓ I practise the teachings of *Velocity Ascension*, a book I channelled from Source that has amazing wisdom and love for the 21st century.
- ✓ I make sure I do my grounding and protection with Archangel Michael at the beginning of the day, and ask to stand in the Golden, Silver, Violet Flame of transmutation.

I've included personal development goals in the same heading, though of course they aren't quite the same. I have read a lot of self-help books in my life and get great nourishment from them. Your personal development goal(s) may relate to something you've always wanted to learn or achieve from self-help books, but your goal may also be related to something you want to be accomplished at!

For instance, one major personal development goal I pursued this year has been participating in ninjutsu classes. Ninjutsu is a martial art that is also deeply spiritual. It is the warrior art of being a 'ninja'. Focused on self-defence, it uses both physical technique and energy from the elements around us:

- Fu – wind
- Ka – Fire
- Sui – Water
- Chi – Earth

The fifth element is Ku – the emptiness or nothingness from which all things assume their form. I always had a secret desire to be a martial arts whiz but never got around to it. At the beginning of the year I asked my son Tariq whether I could improve as a mother in any way. He said, 'Well, Mum, you could be better at martial arts!' A month or so after, a ninjutsu Dojo (school) moved into our local scout hall. This really was the universe at work!

Ninjutsu training has, of course, given me physical confidence – as I can disable even a large, strong man who may be attacking me. Perhaps more importantly, it has given me an invisible *emotional* confidence. It is a part of me realising my Inner Goddess, as Goddesses are by their nature powerful, formidable protectors.

Nurturing Yourself

What many parents fail to do (mothers, in particular) is nurture themselves. They put the needs of children, their spouses, their parents and even their friends before their own needs. One wake-up call I had was the realisation that I'd made these vows to my husband, sealed by a verbal and written marriage contract, and he'd broken nearly all of them. Conversely, I had kept my vows despite being completely un-nurtured in my relationship for years.

How could I make vows to another person and yet treat the most important person in my life so carelessly? Who do I mean by the most important person in my life? I mean *me*. And I say this in a selfless way. The only person guaranteed at your death bed is you – no one else. The only person you can say will unfailingly stay with you throughout your whole life is you. And who do your children have to look after them and help them reach their potential? You!

If my children are to be healthy and happy and flourish, *I* need to be healthy and happy and flourish. My children don't want a miserable mother, a martyr, or someone who is worn down and broken. They need a strong, vibrant mother who can look after their needs because she draws on her own abundance of energy and resilience. They need a mother who rejoices in the joy of life. They need a mother who spreads happiness, calm and love around her. They need me to be present, loving, caring, wise and calm. To be this amazing woman that my children need their mother to be, I need to look after myself – just as you need to look after yourself.

I see so many mothers starve themselves of their own nurturing and make their needs subservient to their children or partners. It can also be the case for fathers – for example, those who work incessantly, or focus on their children's needs at the expense of their own balance. When you have a disabled child to care for, this places an additional burden on you. The burden can be physical – as physically disabled children get older, they can be heavier and more awkward to wash, feed, move, dress. I have put my back out several times lifting Saafi, and hurt my wrists, and he is only five. The emotional burden can also be greater, as we wrestle with the expectations society places on us to be perfect in every way, as well as the emotional demands of managing compromised health, hospital episodes, fear of death or pain for our children.

I have met mothers who have spent whole years in hospital with their children – remarkable women who slept in hospital and rushed to work during the day, then back to hospital at night. But one shouldn't be commended for being a martyr. You deserve a life, because your joy is contagious.

To work out how much you nurture *yourself*, answer the following questions and then add up your scores:

Nurturing Scorecard

How many hours a week do you do exercise? This can be light walking, gym, swimming, yoga, etc.	5 hours: 10 points 3 hours: 5 points 2 hours: 3 points 1 hour or less: 0 points
How many hours a week of meditation do you do?	3 hours: 10 points 1.5 hours: 5 points 0.5 -1.5 hours: 3 points 0.5 hours or less: 0 points
When was the last time you went out with friends on your own?	Last month: 10 Last six months: 2 Last year or longer: 0
How many times a month do you pamper yourself, e.g. get your nails done, go to a spa, go window shopping on your own, put your feet up and read a book, go to a movie?	3x per month or more: 10 points 2x per month or more: 5 points 1x per month: 3 points 0x per month: 0 points
When was the last time you had a night off from caring for your child? (This means the actual night, not just an evening.)	Last month: 10 points Last six months: 5 points Last year: 0 points Never: Subtract 10 points
When was the last time you had a holiday where you could really relax?	Last year: 10 points Last two years: 3 points Not in the last two years: 0 points

Does your diet include a lot of fizzy soft drinks, alcohol and processed food?	Yes: 0 points No: 10 points
When was the last time you were praised?	Today: 10 points In the last two weeks: 5 points In the last month: 2 points Over a month ago: 0 points
When was the last time you told yourself you're doing a good job or praised yourself in some way?	Today: 10 points Within the last week: 8 points Within last 2-4 weeks: 5 points Over a month ago: 0 points
How many hours' sleep do you get a night?	8 hours or more: 10 points 6-7 hours: 5 points 5 hours or less: 0 points
Do you have people around you who regularly use abusive language or actions towards you (at work and/or home)?	Yes: Subtract 20 No: 10

How to interpret your score:

100+

Well done, you! You are generally nurturing yourself well. This will increase your resilience and mean you have good amounts of energy for your disabled child and your other children.

75-100
You've incorporated a good amount of nurturing into your life. Yes, it can be strengthened, but you are generally doing well. Look at ways to increase your score.

50-74
You have some significant drainers in your life and/or lack of attention to your own needs. This presents a risk to yourself and your child. Find ways to increase your score as part of your six-month plan (see end of section).

20-49
You need to take immediate action to nurture yourself more. You risk being a martyr and falling into crisis mode.

19 or Below – Red Flags
It's time to turn things around urgently. You have major deficits in self-nurturing, but you *can* turn this around. It will benefit yourself and your children.

Exercise: Making Vows to Yourself

This is a powerful exercise designed to establish a deep commitment to loving and honouring yourself. Do not make these vows lightly. Take them on as seriously as vows you would commit to for marriage.

1) In your journal, write a list of all the vows you'd like to make to your children. For instance, you may vow to be strong and empowered, healthy, loving and patient.

> 2) Highlight any of these vows that are personally relevant. Would you be comfortable making these vows to yourself?
>
> 3) Write down a list of all the vows you'd like to make to your ideal mate. Perhaps you want to vow to be kind and considerate towards them, to help them fulfil their dreams.
>
> 4) Again, highlight any of these vows that are personally relevant. Would you be comfortable making these vows to yourself?
>
> 5) Are there any vows that you've listed for other people that you don't feel comfortable saying to yourself? If they are wholly positive, what reason could there be for you not to make them to yourself? Do they raise questions of self-love or self-honour?
>
> 6) Combine both lists – the vows you'd make towards your children and those you'd make towards your ideal mate – with those you would like to make to yourself. Add any additional vows that you'd like to make to yourself. All vows should be wholly positive and affirming. Take some time to finalise your list. Reading the list should make you feel great!

For possible inspiration, these are my vows.

I vow to cherish myself.
I vow to nurture my dreams.
I vow to nourish and treasure my body and soul.
I vow to revel in my blessings.

I vow to live life to the full.
I vow to fulfil my potential.
I vow to accept the Goddess and God within me.
I vow to have fun.
I vow to seek wisdom.
I vow to be fearless.
I vow to rejoice in my sexuality.
I vow to forgive myself.

I vow to only keep people in my life who value, honour and nurture me.

I suggest you make a special ceremony or ritual around committing your vows to yourself. This is important because it gives additional emphasis to the vows. It gives your subconscious and conscious mind the clear message that these vows are important to you, because *you* are important.

You could invite some close friends or family to witness these vows to yourself. I chose to be on my own to recite my vows, but I wore a special outfit for the occasion and created a sacred space when I knew I wouldn't be disturbed. It was evening. I lit a candle, performed a special meditation and asked Source (God), the Archangels and other wise beings in the Celestial Kingdom to attend and witness my vows.

I keep my vows in my journal and refer to them when I want a reminder of what I've committed to. You may wish to print or write out your vows and keep them somewhere easy to refer to. You may even wish to frame your vows. Having your vows out in the open could influence how those around you perceive or relate to you, in a positive way. It could also create an inspiration for your children to make vows to themselves. We are teaching our children to live empowered, happy lives, and vows can help us all do that.

Please give this exercise the importance it warrants, and be aware of how your energies towards yourself subsequently shift.

Chapter 6
CAREER & FINANCES

Gosh, this is an area ripe for guilt and various emotions. I recall one excellent article from *The Guardian* that described the emotional burden of being a working mum. It explained that mothers are not only usually responsible for the day-to-day care of the children, but even when the father takes on a major part of the hands-on caregiving, the mother still bears the weight of the administration of the children, e.g. organising the father's involvement, administering the school calendar, events, payments, healthcare, etc. This is a full-time job in itself! Balancing our career aspirations with being a mother or primary caregiver is difficult with healthy children, but when our children are disabled, working takes on a whole new level of considerations. Is a career even possible?

This book places no value judgement on whether it is spiritually better to work or not to work, to pursue a career or not to. You can progress on your spiritual ascension whether a house parent, career parent, or part-time worker. What I assert is the importance of being able to access your own highest guidance to help you navigate the choices you will inevitably have to make as you balance your various needs, desires, dreams and demands.

But after many years of self-exploration, therapy and meditation with my highest guidance, here is what I think on this subject:

- Women and men both have a responsibility to support their children financially. Whilst arrangements can be made for one parent to be the primary financial contributor, it is not *a priori* the right or duty of the father or mother to fulfil this role.
- Women and men have a right to want to pursue their careers. It is not the *a priori* right of the man or the woman to pursue their career at the disadvantage of the other; compromise may be necessary.
- There may be times when children or partners take precedence over careers and vice versa. This is okay.
- The soul contracts we have with our children or partners may not be the most obvious path. What I mean is these relationships were agreed to before we were born. They may not be easy, but there is growth in working through the lessons they present to us.
- For a mother/woman, having a career can be a major energiser and necessary for her to feel fulfilled and happy. The same for a man/father.
- Having a career can enable more opportunities for your child(ren), including your disabled child(ren).

- Choosing a career that is compatible with your childcare preferences may be the best option, e.g. having a job where you work from home or can leave work early to fit around caregiving.
- Having a high-earning job, or ensuring both parents earn, may be the best way to support your children's needs.
- Having time off from childcare to work may be the best option for all members of the family, as this can enable you to energise, fulfil career dreams, have time off from caregiving, and thus increase your appreciation of your children when you are with them.
- It is really important to give your children quality time, dedicated to their needs and desires. Children ideally should have access to both parents. If you give them quality time and love, they will thrive. Money cannot replace quality time with them. This does not mean you have to be there every day of the year – as long as your children know you care and you give them quality time when you can. If you can't be with them all the time, explain why and ensure they know you still love them.
- A healthy balance between our needs and our children's needs, our desires and our children's desires, work, leisure and childcare *is* possible. For me personally, this is key to ensuring a good balance of their financial and emotional security.

Finances can be closely linked to the above considerations, but they are also about the simple fact that we live in the physical earthly world and money is necessary to buy accommodation, food, clothing, healthcare and sometimes schooling and leisure pursuits for our families. Having lived in Africa, I've seen how hard many people work for their children.

Migrant labour is common in Southern African; mothers in lower income households from Zimbabwe, Lesotho and more rural parts of South Africa forfeit living at home with their children to live in cities as domestic workers, cleaners, factory and farm workers, so they can earn better wages to send home to their families, particularly for their children's education and university fees. Sometimes they see their children once per year. This incredible sacrifice is both sad and admirable. Men often make a similar sacrifice.

When we have a disabled child, suddenly our previous financial planning needs to be revisited. Depending on where you live in the world, public healthcare systems will vary. In the UK and America, state care for disabled people can be good and sometimes excellent. In other parts of the world, it might be available through a charity or completely absent.

Usually parents will expect their children to outlive them and to leave home sometime after 18 years of age. Depending on the type and level of disability, this assumption may be completely incorrect. With my beautiful son, whilst I hope to find him a way to be independent as an adult (if he wants to be), he will most likely always need 24-hour care. If he remains in South Africa, any care comes at a cost, so financial planning is essential.

I recommend you think about your financial situation in light of the future life you ideally want for yourself and your children. Being spiritual does not mean being financially negligent. Being spiritual means recognising we live in the earthly plane, being positive and attracting the things we want into our lives through programming ourselves to think with abundance – using affirmations, asking for the support of the angels and celestial kingdom, having a positive attitude to money and taking practical action to save and plan…and really enjoying the financial blessings when they come.

Chapter 7

HEALTH

For many years, I felt I just didn't have enough time to exercise. I had two children, one disabled. I was working all the remaining hours to bring in income that could support our short-term financial needs and allow for longer-term investments, as Saafi needs lifelong care and where we currently live, the state doesn't provide this.

I have never taken my health for granted – I've always eaten healthily, I've never smoked, and I barely touch alcohol. I also seek out the emotions underpinning health troubles, some of which we touch on in this book. But at the beginning of 2018 I felt something wasn't right. I was exhausted all the time. I could barely drag myself through the day. And my hair was falling out – the plug blocked after every hair wash.

A friend of mine mentioned how she'd benefited from going to an integrated health doctor. This physician doesn't just give you a ten-minute once-over and prescribe medicines; (s)he takes one hour to understand the whole you, as well as arranging extensive blood testing to expose any deficiencies you may have in terms of vitamins and hormones.

It was revealing. I was completely depleted in vitamin D, B-vitamins and progesterone. The primary cause was chronic stress, most probably caused by a six-week health scare from Saafi earlier that year (when he developed epilepsy), years of verbal aggression from my partner, and a demanding five years coming to terms with disability, divorce and major money worries. This was causing my adrenalin to work overtime and depleting me to the breaking point. My doctor also advised me to take up Pilates or some muscle-building activity to counteract the aging process and further improve my overall health.

This is a good illustration of how it is essential to look after yourself. How can you look after your children or others when you have no energy left to move –when you are clinically burnt out? It also underscores how essential it is to understand the way stressors impact your body, not just in the short term but in the medium or long term. The cumulative impact of stress or lack of self-nurturing can be disastrous. My doctor said that with the stresses I'd been under so consistently for so many years, he was amazed I hadn't suffered a far more serious health collapse or disease.

Our own thoughts, and the thoughts and words others direct at us, can affect our health, on top of the experiences and stresses of life and having a disabled child. But your health is of primary importance to your children. If you want to look after them, you *need* to put in place actions that nurture and energise you, both mentally and physically.

What I realised was the need to:

a) take supplements that restored my body to optimum health;
b) strengthen my physical body (increase muscle-to-fat ratio) to prevent future health challenges as I get older and, importantly, enable me to lift Saafi as he gets heavier, without putting my back out;
c) continue to protect myself spiritually against negative thoughts – especially from my ex, but also from my own self-doubt;

and, importantly,

d) re-programme my brain to attract what I was currently lacking.

An unexpected end to my work contract gave me time to invest in my health. For me, this was an example of how the universe creates the space for you to do what you need to do, if you don't create the space yourself. With an abundance of time – something I complained I always lacked – I got myself organised, joined a gym and enrolled with a personal trainer, taking advantage of a special of three free sessions.

It is incredible what I've achieved in just those three months, with the help of my dedicated and inspiring trainer, Ernest. I've gained an extra kilogram of muscle. Far from looking like a female body builder, I just look a bit trimmer. Tariq was always asking me to get fitter and stronger so he could race against me, swim with me and be carried by me. He loves that I can now carry him – a ten-year-old – with ease on my back, an accomplishment I am quite proud of.

But the person who really notices the difference is *me*. I can walk upstairs without puffing, hold Saafi more easily, and I haven't put my back out recently, as the muscle strength in my core body is improved. It's given me greater confidence in all areas of my life. I feel great!

A number of years ago I learnt that my body parts (brain, liver, knees, feet, ankles, spine, etc.) each have personalities and will communicate their welfare directly to me, if I only have the patience to listen. New biological evidence is now becoming public to explain the science underpinning how each cell has a 'mind' and, therefore, why we shouldn't dismiss the possibility of our body parts talking to us[2].

I check in regularly with my body and take on its recommendations; it could be getting myself to the doctor, or kinesiologist, getting more sleep, taking more of a specific supplement, or relaxing more.

The following meditation, whilst important if you have a health problem afflicting a particular body part, is a powerful tool for getting in touch with your body and learning to communicate with it. If you practise checking in with your body in this way, you'll become experienced at picking up the needs of your body and mind before serious health problems occur. You'll also get better at feeling great more quickly, as long as you take whatever action your body advises.

---

[2]   Bruce Lipton, *The Biology of Belief*

Visualisation to Connect with a Dis-eased Body Part

Close your eyes. Feel your feet on the floor. Imagine tiny golden roots growing out of the soles of your feet and into the magical soil of the Earth.

Become aware of your breathing. As you breathe in, imagine an amazing white light filling your body. As you breathe out, imagine tiny golden stars exploding from the top of your head. You are calm and relaxed. Continue this cleansing breath for a few minutes.

Imagine you are in a beautiful field. Butterflies flit in the air, the sun is warm on your skin, the birds are singing, and the field is bursting with red poppies and yellow sunflowers.

In front of you appears a beautiful angel. It is Archangel Chamuel, the angel of love. You greet Chamuel and tell her you are having health problems with [body part or issue]. You ask if she can help.

She walks over to you and lays her hand on the part of your body that is hurting or dis-eased. She presses her other hand to your ear.

She says that by her touching your ear and your troubled body part, you will be able to hear that part speak. It will tell you directly the root cause of the ailment. Listen carefully to what your body part says. It may reveal the root cause is an emotion or an experience. Whatever it says, listen and accept this.

Now Chamuel touches her hand to your heart chakra, and you feel it fill with warm, energising, nurturing love. This love fills your heart chakra to the brim, so it flows out of your heart chakra and throughout your body, throughout your aura, into your brain and legs and feet and arms and hands, until you are flooded with the most amazing pink energy of love.

Now Chamuel asks you to send love to the body part that is troubling you. You do this by directing the love energy in your heart chakra to your suffering body part. As you do so, you tell it you love it: 'I love you. I love you. Thank you for being you. Thank you for being part of my beautiful body.' For your body is a gift and the more you love it, the more it will respond well for you.

Archangel Chamuel says she will always be with you to give you love and help you love your body. You thank her.

Wiggle your toes and fingers, shrug your shoulders and return to the room. Write down in your journal any thoughts or messages you received from your body.

Chapter 8
FINDING THE PLATINUM LINING

Finding the platinum lining (PL) is a combination of practising the habit of happiness (HH) and getting a clearer understanding of your soul purpose (SP):

$$PL = HH + SP$$

Practising the habit of happiness is about finding the joy in small things. For instance, when Saafi was in intensive care and I was surviving on about three hours sleep a night, I would take moments on my way home from the hospital to appreciate the glory of the purple jacaranda tree blooms that lined the street. I do the same in my garden – taking in frangipani flowers and their sensual scent, scarlet hibiscus blooms – or in walking in my Cornish moorland.

If I catch sight of a special bird, I similarly give thanks for this beauty and grace in nature. For instance, one day a kingfisher came and balanced on the umbrella outside my little property in Cornwall. Its iridescent blue, streamlined beak were mesmerising up close. These shy birds are rarely seen.

I focus on the sensations I am feeling at that moment. I release the need to dwell on my worries, on what has happened in the past, and any worries about the future. I just allow my senses to take in the beauty around me.

I repeat this habit throughout the day with everyday delights. For instance, I pause to allow the nectar of freshly squeezed orange run over my tongue. I play an uplifting song. I experience the joy of my children's love for one another, or the softness of their hair and skin. I take joy from the delight Tariq has in his friends or when he scores well at school. I equally celebrate when Saafi manages to grab my hair, laughs and giggles, or visually demonstrates his adoration of ice cream.

Giving Thanks

Giving thanks is an essential part of the habit of happiness. It's easy to dwell on what we don't have, what we haven't achieved in life or what we still hanker for. It's okay to want more and strive for more, but it's essential to pause and take stock of what we have.

There are so many things to be thankful for. This could be our health, our eyesight, hearing, having an income, a nice day trip we've had, an outing to the cinema, a nice meal, a new garment, a great book we've read, close friends and love of family, and of course our children. Every night before my elder son goes to sleep (he's currently 10), we lie in bed and say thank you for three lovely things that have happened throughout the day. I also often just give thanks during the day and will say out loud, 'Thank you for my beautiful home', or 'Thank you for my wonderful children'.

And I thank both my children to their faces and tell them how lucky I am that they are in my life. 'Thank you, Tariq, for being such a kind, loving, attentive brother to Saafi. And thank you for being such a loving and helpful son to me'. 'Thank you Saafi for being such a brave, strong boy and being so kind, and giving so much love and fun to everyone around you'.

Even if Saafi cannot speak or respond yet, I believe he understands what I say. If you have a child who cannot communicate in the same way an able-bodied child does, I think it's important we treat them the age they are and assume they are fully cognitively able. There have been so many examples of children written off as having subnormal IQ just because their physical bodies are severely disabled and then in later life they've found a way to communicate (such as through eye computers) and they have turned out to be exceptionally bright. Never underestimate your child.

Even with children with severe learning disabilities, speak to them with warm words. Their subconscious may well understand. Tell them they're smart, and measure them by their own standards, and not those of others. I give thanks that Saafi can grab my hair, sometimes with multiple attempts, and I say thank you everyday that he laughs and enjoys life.

Remember: if you derive joy from your child, he or she will feel it.

Giving Back

Giving back is so important to send the message to the universe you are committed to others and not just yourself, as well as recognizing that money, time, love, abundance is a 'flow' when you give, knowing you deserve, it will come back to you a thousand-fold. It can be little things, smiling at people, trying to make someone's day a little better. It can be giving back to someone including those you wouldn't normally help, or it can be giving back on a wider or grander scale. Giving back doesn't need to be giving money to charity; it could be giving your time or your ideas to a worthy cause, perhaps through your job. Giving back can be incredibly rewarding.

Colour

The habit of happiness is finding joy even in the smallest things, even when everything around you appears calamitous. I even take joy from a vibrantly coloured towel!

Colour is worth a special mention in the habit of happiness. There is a whole science on colour therapy. Different colours have different effects on your mind, body and aura. The more difficult my life has seemed, the brighter my clothing or furnishings around me have tended to become. I love vibrant blues, magentas, scarlets and emerald greens – animal prints and sequins – and I particularly love gold!

I love gold hats and handbags and shoes. Not only is gold a beautiful, gleaming, heart-warming colour, but it is also a spiritual colour. It is the colour of the chakras in the 7th dimension (rose gold, peach gold, shimmering or sequined gold, etc.) and has been a spiritual colour in most cultures throughout millennia – for a reason.

When I wear my gold-sequined cap, my heart immediately feels lighter. And I make so many interesting acquaintances when I wear it! I get approached on the street, in the airport, when I'm sitting on benches in London. People say, 'Hi! I love your hat'. And we start chatting. I got photographed by the world-renowned Cambodian artist, Milan Rai, who photographs people with white butterflies of peace, throughout the world – just because of my gold sequined hat! He saw me sitting on a bench and gazing at the Thames, whilst I was waiting for a friend to finish work. He approached and asked if he could take a photo of me holding two beautiful, white paper butterflies.

I don't always want to be as flamboyant as my gold hat makes me, but I still have my gleaming gold handbags, which make me smile whenever I pick them up. I also have a luxurious crimson crushed velvet window seat in my white kitchen, with crushed velvet gold cushions and sparkling diamante crystal tiles around the walls. I've had children stare in wonder at these crystals and tell each other I have diamonds in my walls. For me, my gold and glittering objects symbolise hope, joy, aspiration, abundance, financial security, and fun. They lift my vibrations and add 'colour' to my life.

There is a wealth of literature on colour therapy. I encourage you to experiment with different colours in your dress and furnishings and see how they make you feel. In Appendix 6, I have included a table of colours in the 3rd and 7th dimensions and the Archangels that work with these colours. I invite you to bring these colours into your life. The wonderful gleaming and sequined golds, iridescent blues and greens, gleaming silver and diamante will make you feel uplifted! Consult this table when you follow the exercise below.

Experiment with these colour therapies:

1) Make yourself a rose petal bath, and add rose essential bath oil.
2) Cover an old or drab couch in a vibrant colour that makes your heart sing.
3) Buy yourself a gold handbag, key ring or purse. When you use it, think of abundance and joy.

4) Each day of the week, experiment wearing a different colour of outfit. How do the colours make you feel?
5) Buy a brightly coloured garment in a colour you wouldn't normally wear. How does it make you feel?
6) Buy or pick yourself flowers that make your heart zing, and put them somewhere in your house where you will see them a lot.
7) Experiment with sumptuously coloured fruit, vegetables and recipes. Make a meal for yourself that is a colour therapy delight:

- Strawberries and cream
- Watermelon salad (with sliced red onion, feta cheese cubes, black pepper, and a lime and olive oil dressing)
- Carrot and orange soup with homemade beetroot bread
- Blackberry and apple crumble with runny cream
- Fresh carrot juice, beetroot juice, strawberry juice, orange juice, or blueberry and banana smoothie!

8) Paint yourself a colour-feeling painting. Buy a blank canvas of whatever size you choose. Experiment with bright colours, bold textures, glitter, stars, and even positive words like 'love', 'happy', 'joy'.
9) Fill coloured glass bottles with filtered water, leave them for a day to infuse the energy of the colour of the bottle, and then enjoy the calming effect it has on you.

Chapter 9
THE POWER OF WORDS

'Bricks and stones may break my bones, but words will never hurt me'.

People often recited the above phrase to me, to try to give me strength to get through the pain of being in a verbally abusive relationship. But the truth is, words *do* hurt and there is now evidence to show that verbal abuse, including shouting and insults, have a detrimental *physical* as well as emotional impact on people. My fading health and my medical exhaustion were directly linked by my physician to my draining relationship and the constant 'fight or flight' reflex my body instinctively activated through an injection of adrenalin into the blood stream when I was being shouted at and my body was screaming, 'Danger... danger!'

In her new book *Dodging Energy Vampires*, Dr Christine Northrup links disease and depleted health directly to similar relationships to mine. I stayed in my marriage thinking it was the best thing I could do for my children, but when I realised the damage it was causing, I left. My children are confirmation I did the right thing. Today, they are buoyantly happy. They still see both parents, but they are no longer subjected to a toxic environment.

In the UK, verbal and emotional abuse is a documented form of domestic abuse. Regular shouting around babies changes their brain wave patterns. Research coming out of Colombia University has linked household domestic abuse to the likelihood of war and instability. Even children who protect their abused mothers from abusive fathers have often been found to go on to be abusers themselves.

Being surrounded by violence, no matter what form, changes brains; and whilst the damage can be undone, it takes a conscious effort. It is better to avoid the situation, address it or get our children out. If you are in a relationship anything like my own, I encourage you to consider the impact on your children, as well as on yourself.

I was particularly moved by evidence generated by the Japanese scientist, Dr Masaru Emoto, who spent much of his career experimenting with the effect that various words, music and colours can have on water molecules. A revolutionary thinker, Emoto discovered that kind words versus ugly words fundamentally change the structure of water. For instance, in one of his experiments he put rice and water in three different glass beakers. For one month he said to the first jar, 'Thank you.' To the second beaker, he said, 'I hate you'. He ignored the third jar.

After one month, the first jar had fermented and was sweet smelling. The second jar had turned black and the third jar was rotten. He found that under a microscope, when he froze each of these jars of water, the molecules of the water that had been told the words 'love' and 'gratitude' developed splendid symmetrical structures.

Water that was told 'hate' or 'idiot' turned into irregular structures.

What is the importance of this information? Well, we are 60% water – so his findings suggest that the impact of words on the water in our bodies has a direct effect on our health and tendency to disease in our bodies. Remember: the words you say to your children (or others) impact them – not just their brains but the physical water of their bodies. The words other people say to them also have an effect. Surround your child with loving people and words; this will help your children's health and happiness.

This includes limiting words, such as, 'My son can't walk. He'll never be able to walk'. Replace this with, 'My son isn't able to walk *yet*. But he is capable of many wonderful things and constantly amazes me'. Use reinforcing words for your disabled child. 'She is so brave, she is so strong, she is so smart, she is so loving!' 'I am proud of you'. And be mindful of the things you say to your disabled child's siblings. The soul contract does not exist only between you and your children; it is also very strong between your children!

I've been very careful in Saafi's life to encourage my elder son's natural inclination to roll and bear play with Saafi. Saafi adores it. The knee-jerk reaction can be to wrap our special children in cotton wool. We worry they are weak and need to be protected, but keeping their siblings at a distance from them can create a tension and resentment that sometimes never heals. Tariq and Saafi now have such a tight bond and such exquisite unconditional love for one another that it is a joy to witness. They considerably enrich each other's lives. I regularly praise Tariq for how he cares for Saafi: 'Tariq, you are such a loving brother to Saafi. He is so lucky to have you in his life'. And I also praise Saafi: 'Saafi, you are such a brave, loving boy and give everyone around you so much love. We are so lucky to have you in our lives'.

And let's not forget ourselves! When was the last time you said nice things to yourself? Sometimes I look in the mirror and I say, 'I love you, Hele', or, 'You are an amazing being, Hele'. I also thank my body. It is my vessel, it is my friend, and each part of my body plays a special role in enriching my life. When I was expressing breast milk for Saafi, I would thank my breasts and tell them I loved them. And it made them feel good.

It is also really important to be aware of all the judgement we pick up from those around us. Saying wonderful things to ourselves is a way of counteracting negative thoughts we may inadvertently pick up from other people. It's not about ego and saying, 'Look at me – I'm just so amazing!' It's about honouring ourselves.

The Power of Thoughts

Remember that the words you say to yourself impact your body! I learned this in a transformational training in Australia about 20 years ago.

I mentioned earlier that I am a trained Kahuna masseuse. The internationally renowned Kahuna teacher Mette Sorensen ran the first level training that I attended. It was held beside the beach, near Sydney, with an eclectic group of participants from whom I learnt many lessons.

In one of the exercises, we gathered in a room and one volunteer – let's call her Sue – was asked to wait outside until she was called back in. When Sue had left, Mette told the rest of us that we were participating in an experiment and gave us our instructions.

When Sue came back into the room, Mette asked her to hold her arm out straight in front of her body. Another member of the audience – let's call him Tom – was asked to stand beside Sue and push down on that arm. Tom pushed down, but Sue's arm held strong and straight.

On the first signal from Mette we, the audience, had to think beautiful, loving thoughts about Sue. We had to think how lovely she looked, how nice her clothes were, what a great person she was, how much we liked her. Tom pressed down on her arm, but it remained strong, barely wavering under his pressure.

Mette gave a second signal. As instructed, this time we sent nasty thoughts to Sue. We imagined she was ugly, a despicable person whom we despised. Her arm just sank under Tom's pressure on it, as if she had no strength to hold it up at all.

On the third signal Mette made, once again we thought beautiful thoughts about Sue, as many lovely things as we could imagine. Her arm held strong and straight just like on the first signal.

In a life-transforming moment, this revealed to me just how important it is to herd our thoughts! These thoughts directly affected Sue's physical strength, without the words even being spoken aloud. This demonstrated to me that thoughts have power – on others and ourselves. Outstanding authors, Lynne McTaggart and Dr Bruce Lipton, have now proven this scientifically. Be aware of your thoughts with yourself and your children.

The Ego

Beware of the ego. This is our conscious mind, driven by fears and lack of comprehension that we are one with the Divine. It is the obstacle we need to overcome, having accepted the Veil of Amnesia upon entering the Earth in physical form. Our ego will chide us for not having the best job/house/income/beauty. When we become aware of a voice in our heads chiding us, we have become aware of our ego and that our essence – our 'I AM' – is separate from the ego. This awareness is very powerful because we can then start turning the negative chides of the ego into positive affirmations of who we are and what we can become.

The ego might say, 'You'll never be able to make a successful go of that shop. You're too disorganised/stupid/unlucky/unsupported....' The 'I AM' can then step in and counter this with, 'I run a successful shop because I'm wise, supported and organised'. In this way, we can manifest abundance in our life.

Be aware of why you want something. Do you want a promotion because it will make you feel that you are as good or better than your friends/colleagues/peers/others? Or a new house because it will affirm that you are doing well in life? 'Things' feed the ego's need to feel superior and fears of not being worthy/loved/good enough. Be aware of criticising, being angry and judging others, things and situations – slating politicians, certain individuals, and even whole cultures/races. By slating others, we put them down and feed our ego's need to feel superior.

Collective ego is one of the most destructive forces on the planet. This is where whole groups of people, sometimes whole nations, justify extreme behaviour because of the 'wrongness' of others and the 'rightness' of their own views. Religious wars and national conflicts have been built on this type of superiority. Force is sometimes necessary to protect oneself, but we should still try to do it from a position of unconditional love, looking for possible evidence in ourselves of behaviours demonstrated in our opponents, who are often the mirrors to our own inner world. If we change our perspective on a person, they may well change their perspective on us. They will subconsciously pick up on the energetic change when we change our outlook.

Do not think that if you say sweet things to your partner/boss, but denigrate them behind their back or subconsciously, they won't pick up on it. They will feel it subconsciously and respond. Every thought you have creates a reaction – unless you call in the Golden, Silver, Violet Flame, with the underlying aim of unconditional love.

Unconditional Love and the Self

Unconditional love is one of the most important laws of the universe. When we love someone unconditionally, we love them without (for example) requiring them to love us back or respond in a certain way. If we find ourselves withholding affection because our friend/colleague/lover/child hasn't behaved the way we want them to, even using our affection as a bartering tool, we are placing conditions on our love.

Loving unconditionally also means we love someone whatever their imperfections. We step forward along our spiritual path and recognise the Divine that is in everyone. We look for and see the 'Godspark' within us all. We recognise the fundamental truth that we are all connected to God/Source and there is a pure part of us, the essence of all that is good about us, that is intrinsically lovable.

Angels vibrate at a very high frequency – the seventh dimension and above – and are beings of pure love and light. Whatever we do, they will not judge us, or condemn us, or dislike us; they will continue to love us and shower us with blessings.

As we raise our vibrations from the third to the fourth through to the seventh dimension (the dimension of angels, Ascended Masters and other beings of light, such as unicorns), the lessons of our heart chakra evolve. In the fifth dimension, where we master unconditional love, we may love a person unconditionally, but this does not mean we have to 'like' them or the behaviours they exhibit. It is intrinsically linked to 'respect' and being 'non-judgemental'.

I may not like everyone in my workplace, but I aim to respect them as fellow human beings and recognise the Godspark within each of them.

I may not like what a murderer has done, but whilst a retribution system within society is necessary, I leave the ultimate judgement to God; for we do not know what is in the soul contract of the murderer.

Unconditional love is not an easy lesson to master. If someone has deeply hurt us or people we love, it can be incredibly difficult to forgive them; but remember, we don't have to learn to like them, just to recognise that however deeply buried, there is a piece of God within everyone.

One of the most difficult lessons for us all in human form is to love *ourselves* unconditionally. We are born into Earth with the Veil of Amnesia – without the memory that we are part of Source and perfectly formed in each lifetime to learn the lessons we need to progress along our spiritual path. The lessons we choose are usually specifically set up to introduce feelings of worthlessness, rejection and fear.

To overcome this, we must realise our intrinsic perfection, connectedness to Source and divine lovability. Until we do, our lives will be characterised in one way or another by failed relationships, or relationships where we do not feel fully loved and valued, or experiences where we feel rejected, victimised or vulnerable.

Know that the answer is within. Until we love ourselves unconditionally, others around us will not love us unconditionally. Do not look for proof of lovability around you. Love yourself unconditionally and you will find an endless affirmation of your lovability around you. How do we do this?

1) Everyday look in the mirror and say, 'Hello, Amazing Being'.
2) Look for and understand the patterns in your life.
3) Forgive yourself your imperfections by recognising you are perfect in these imperfections.
4) Radiate love to yourself. Imagine the feeling you get when you are falling in love, and radiate that energy to your own heart.
5) Visualise your inner child. Hold, love and protect that child, and reassure them of their lovability
6) When you catch yourself criticising yourself, replace this with a positive affirmation. For instance, if you find yourself saying, 'I am so stupid – how could I have done that?" replace it immediately with, 'I forgive myself and recognise my divine lovability'.
7) Repeat the Forgiveness Creed below, regularly or daily for 30 days. This helps you learn to forgive yourself and others.
8) Ask to work with Archangel Chamuel, who guards the heart chakra and leads the angels of love; Archangel Zadkiel, who commands the Golden, Silver, Violet Flame; the angels of for-

giveness; and, of course, your own Guardian Angel. (See Appendix 2)
9) Repeat 'I AM' mantras: 'I AM unconditional love – I AM the Golden, Silver Violet Flame'. (See Appendix 2)
10) Laugh, have innocent/joyful fun, nurture and honour yourself. (Do not be a martyr – this is especially important for women!)
11) Perform yoga, Kahuna dancing, or other forms of body integration.
12) Massage heart chakra angel oils into the heart chakra.

Forgiveness Creed

I forgive all others for any harm they've done to me in this life, or previous lives, in this world, the Universe or any dimension.

I forgive myself for any harm I've done to another person, animal or thing in this life, or previous lives, in this world, the Universe or any dimension.

I forgive myself for any harm I've done to myself and for all my imperfections and failings, in this life and previous lives, in this world, the Universe or any dimension.

I choose to be a being of unconditional love and light and to love myself unconditionally, knowing that by seeking to be on my best and highest path I am serving the world.

Visualisation to Bring in Unconditional Love with Lady Gaia

This is a wonderful meditation that will leave you uplifted and at peace. Lady Gaia is the protectress of the Earth. She is a powerful, grounded and wise celestial being, full of patience and love. In this meditation she uses fruit from her etheric retreat (energy home) to heal and power your heart and make it flow with unconditional love (love without judgement).

Prepare yourself for meditation. Sit or lie down, close your eyes, and ground and protect yourself.

You find yourself in the most exquisite of gardens. This is Lady Gaia's garden. It is full of bright blooming flowers, in artistically designed flowerbeds. Stately fountains spray pink-gold water to the heavens that falls in fine mist into the fountain pools. Fruit trees line the paths that weave around the fountains and flowerbeds. The garden is alive with bees, birds and butterflies.

The sun is warm on your skin and you sit on one of the many polished wood benches in the garden.

Towards you walks a beautiful woman wearing a simple dress of pink and green silk. Her feet are bare. She is Lady Gaia. Upon her head is a woven crown of white flowers. The closer she gets, the more you feel loved, valued and safe.

She now stands in front of you. She speaks to you and her words form inside your heart: *I am love and I am here to give you the gift of unconditional love. Will you accept my gift?* You nod, as you are very happy to receive this gift.

She plucks a fruit that you do not know the name for, from a tree with emerald green leaves and pink-gold flowers. The fruit are balls of pink-gold light. She tells you this is one of her many fruit trees of love. She presses the fruit towards your heart chakra in the centre of your chest. The pink-gold light of the fruit is absorbed into your body and you instantly feel love for yourself and everything in the world. She keeps her hand on the centre of your chest and the feeling increases in power, filling your whole body. You feel able to solve the world's challenges as well as your own.

This is the fruit of unconditional love, she says, and it is here for you whenever your heart is sore or you need additional love and strength in your life. The fruits are abundant and grow everywhere in this garden. You know you can return whenever you wish. You know you are loved, you love unconditionally, and you are powerful and resilient in the face of challenges. You know you are safe.

You thank Lady Gaia.

When you are ready, rub your hands together, shrug your shoulders and come back to the room.

Exercise: Learning to Love Yourself

1) Each day, practise saying to yourself, 'I love you, [name]. You're doing really well, [name]'.
2) Every day, thank your body or a particular body part for the contribution they are making to your day.
3) Herd your thoughts. Be conscious of all the negative words or messages you are directing at yourself every day. Are you chastising yourself that you haven't done well enough? Or telling yourself you're an idiot, or a poor mother or poor father, or not good enough at work, or failing your potential?

Turn those messages around. Write down all the negative words or messages you tell yourself in the left-hand column of a page. On the right-hand side, write down the opposite of those messages. Below, I have shared some examples. You will see that sometimes I use the first person ('I') and sometimes I use the second person ('you').

Old Thought Pattern	New Thought Pattern
I'm a bad mother. I'm not doing enough for my child(ren).	I'm the best mother I can be now. I am doing well.
Idiot.	I love you.
You're useless.	You're really able.
You're the worst parent this child could have.	This child has chosen me at a soul level and I am doing the best I can in the situation. I forgive myself for any imperfections.
I am trapped.	I am free.
I am a failure.	I am a success.
Life is a slog.	There is something amazing in every day.

Repeat the new thought pattern and allow yourself to swell with joy at how it makes you feel to experience this new way of thinking. For instance, if you're thinking, 'I am free', how does it *feel* to be really free? Allow your imagination to flow, and make the feelings as real as you can.

A particularly powerful time to repeat these positive affirmations is before you go to sleep. You can also record them and replay them as you fall asleep each night. This self-hypnosis influences the subconscious mind, which is 95% of where our thoughts come from.

Over the weeks of repeating these new thought patterns, note how your emotions change. On a scale of 1-10 measure your level of vibrancy, e.g. 10 means you feel really vibrant, 1 means you feel terrible. Don't judge yourself if you have an up week or month, and then a down week or month. That's life. Just look for the general trend.

Chapter 10
FAMILY & FRIENDS

Many of us have obligations broader than our children. We might look after elderly parents, or maybe we have dependent siblings. But our children will play a significant role in the goals we choose in this section.

These visualisations will help you think out of the box for your disabled child. Rather than putting limitations on what your disabled child can achieve, remind yourself that they have a soul contract; if they don't achieve the milestones that you would ideally love them to, don't be dispirited – it may just be their soul contract playing out.

There are constantly new technologies and scientific discoveries that could help improve the outcome for our disabled children. The invention of eye-controlled computer technology has meant many children and adults who previously couldn't communicate, as they were unable to speak or write, can now communicate through controlling text on a computer screen with their eyes. This is life-changing.

There are no limits. Encourage and support your child to reach their full potential, and be happy, content and proud of them for whatever they do achieve. Saafi can't yet talk, but he can communicate his needs very well through his own noises and facial gestures. We are hoping one day he will be able to control his eyes well enough to use an eye computer. We are hoping that with the help of a gait trainer and ABR therapy, one day he will walk. But if he doesn't manage this, it won't limit my pride in him or the joy in having him in our lives.

Our role at a spiritual level is to support our children on their best and highest path (what they were put on this planet to learn), to learn from them, and to co-create happiness with them.

Remembering Your Other Children

It is easy when you have a disabled child, especially if you are their main caregiver, to divert the balance of time and effort to that child. But our other children need just as much attention.

My elder son, Tariq, is very vocal and it hit home to me one day when he said, 'Mum you just give Saafi all the attention'. When we started the ABR treatment, I began giving it myself to Saafi. It is intense, requiring up to three hours per day. Tariq began to play up and interfere with the therapy. I realised Tariq needs as much attention as Saafi. For me, this meant a profound rethink in how I divide my time and attention between the two boys. I must treat them as individuals, not as a package. Whilst they adore each other, Saafi also likes to share a bed with me and not share me with Tariq. Yet, Tariq also wants a night with me.

THE SPIRITUAL SIDE OF DISABILITY

So I put in place the following actions to give them both what I felt they needed:

- Separate holiday time for Tariq and separate time with Saafi (for instance, when the boys' father takes Tariq)
- Together time for both – together holidays and outings
- At least one night for each a week in my bed, to have me to themselves
- I've taken tennis lessons so I can play with Tariq
- I play Scrabble and chess and paint with Tariq
- I take Saafi for ice cream outings alone
- I read to Saafi
- I do Tariq's homework with him
- I go to the cinema with Tariq
- I've taken up ninjutsu at Tariq's request and take him to classes sometimes
- I make cakes with the boys and feed Saafi cake mixture – he loves this
- I take Saafi swimming
- I play ball and race with Tariq in the pool separately from Saafi
- I trampoline with Saafi and Tariq, sometimes together and sometimes separately
- I ask Tariq questions and listen to his answers, and separately do the same for Saafi

If you have more than one child, I encourage you to give them individual time. During the times you spend with other children, someone will need to be with your disabled child. Do not feel guilty. Ask for help, from family, friends or public/charity support. One of the lessons of disabled children is to allow yourself to be supported.

Paying for someone's time can also an option. It is an investment in yourself and your family.

Your Children's Relationship with Each Other

At a spiritual level, the relationship between siblings is very significant. The relationship between able-bodied and disabled children is equally significant. They have a soul contract with each other, just like you have a soul contract with your children. There are lessons for each of them to learn, challenges and opportunities to experience, karma to repay and soul families to share this incarnation with.

I've mentioned this elsewhere, but try not to wrap your disabled children in cotton wool, and be really careful not to tell off your able-bodied children for playing with their disabled sibling. Sure, you have to keep a careful eye, but if your fear and protective instinct for your disabled child create tension for your other children when they seek to play, it can drive a wedge between them that will last forever. Work at finding that balance between empowering your able-bodied child(ren) and protecting your disabled child.

Tariq found my limit when I walked in on him swinging Saafi upside down by his feet – Tariq was about seven and Saafi two! But I playfully educated him in how to hold Saafi while still supporting their rough-and-tumble, as I realised both siblings adore this physical interaction. For children who can't walk or even roll themselves, having a sibling to roll with, tickle them, and lay them on a trampoline and bounce them gently, this is absolute bliss.

Tariq also took delight in patting Saafi on his nose. Sometimes it seemed too hard to me, but Saafi would break into uncontrolled giggles, so I allowed myself to go with the flow.

Nurture the relationship they have and empower your able-bodied children in their interactions. Tell them how caring, devoted, loving, wonderful and patient they are with their siblings and how proud you are of them. This will make them treasure the relationship with their disabled siblings, rather than fear it or see it as a cause of their own castigation.

Allow Your Able-Bodied Children to Be Carefree

In my experience, able-bodied children often absorb a massive amount of turbulence and emotional pain from their parents. This can be as a bystander or sometimes as a punching bag, either physical or emotional.

Whilst we as parents are going through the shock, trauma, fear, guilt and sometimes anger and depression of coming to terms with disability, our children not only live in the emotional stew but they can also take the brunt of this pain. Parents have their own coping mechanisms, but sometimes when depression sets in, they just don't cope. Those around them take in this trauma. Whilst adults can hopefully rationalise the emotions at play, children often can't. They accept it, but often it can lead to trauma, stress, and behavioural problems.

It is often easy to forget that our older able-bodied children also had expectations of what their new sibling would be like, and they may need help adjusting to the new situation. If the disabled child is the older child, the able-bodied children will be born into the situation – this is their normal. But we still need to create an environment for them that enables them to blossom and reach their highest potential.

One way of doing this is to allow your able-bodied children to feel free to have time on their own with their own friends, not being the caregiver, a role they sometimes lapse into and, when we need help sometimes, a role we encourage. Let them have joy, re-energise and get out of the worry-energy that can surround disability. Let them be children too, free from guilt or worry.

Relationships

So often when we have children, our relationship with our mate becomes secondary. It gets displaced and we function with the children at the centre of our lives. I've seen couples lose themselves in their children, and when those children eventually leave home the parents are lost, unclear of what they have in common and sometimes why they are even together.

When you add disability into the mix, the relationship with your mate can become even more challenged. I often think of a marriage like a vase – if there are cracks before a trauma, challenges can cause the cracks to be extenuated. But if the vase (or relationship) is strong, it can become stronger with the new situation.

A Stronger Relationship

I met an inspiring mum who has a beautiful little girl with a chromosome deficiency. The girl can't close her eyes or sit, speak or bend; she's like a little doll. The mum was so in love with this little girl, it was beautiful to witness. She said that she and her husband, who had several other able-bodied children, had been going through a rocky patch before their daughter was born, but this had brought them together and the mum was happier than she'd ever been.

Honour the relationship you have with your partner and don't take it for granted. Go on date nights – find someone who will care for your children, take advantage of care that may be offered by the government, or pay for professional help if necessary. Even if it is just one night per year, investing in your relationship is an investment in your children. Remember: if their parents are happy, they will flourish with this energy.

Finding a New Special Other

If you are a single parent, father or mother, in a family including a disabled child, this section is also where you include your hopes and dreams for a new mate, a fulfilling, loving partner who respects you and honours your children.

Finding a mate when you already have children can be daunting. Our negative egos can send us negative messages. This is the voice in your mind that says you are not good enough – why would anyone want to go out with you? You can't find someone who will love your children as much as they need to be loved, and to be allowed into your life. I have also been told that hardly any man would go out with a woman with disabled children. What rubbish!

Be very careful what messages you surround yourself with. If we love ourselves, there will be someone out there who loves us well. And importantly, if someone is worth loving, they will embrace our beautiful children as the gifts they are. I have been very careful throughout my life to surround myself with positive messages and positive, loving people. If people continually drain, demean and disempower me, I let them go. Life is too short to waste on negative people. We can have everything we want. We just need to ask and be open to it. Practise the habit of happiness and you will be amazed how much wonder flows into your life. If you want a new mate, put that request out there to the universe.

Knowing When to Let Go

One intuitive friend received a message for me from her spiritual guides. The message was that Saafi was my 'portal'. I had also received a similar message. Saafi allowed me to leave a troubled and emotionally abusive marriage. Whilst my husband had periods of being supportive and charming, he was very controlling and if I didn't do exactly what he wanted, he would punish me with aggressive shouting, rages and name calling, or by emotionally withdrawing from me, sometimes for weeks or even months. This could be over minor things like forgetting an old blanket at a friend's house, or offering to take the family on a recharging holiday. He seemed unaware of the impact of his behaviour on me, and on the children.

He also blamed me for Saafi's cerebral palsy, although there was no medical basis for the accusation. I have heard of many instances where the father has abandoned the family because of the birth of a disabled child. Our children are blessed, because whatever faults my husband may have, our children have two devoted parents to love and support them.

Whilst I acknowledge the commitment and devotion my children's father has to both of them, I couldn't give my children the energy they needed whilst also withstanding the damaging emotions he brought into the household. I realised it was negatively affecting my children, and family and friends helped convince me I had to leave for my children's sake and for my own. Having Saafi ultimately showed me the way to a happier state of being.

Chapter 11
DRAINERS & ENERGISERS

Below is an amazing exercise you can do to understand who the energisers or drainers in your life are. It can also help identify people you know to help you realise certain specific goals, as well as individuals you need to bring into your life to get from A (where you currently are) to B (where you want to be).

What is an energiser? An energiser is a person who makes you feel good, strong and 're-energised' when you're with them. A drainer is someone who leaves you feeling depleted, tired, weaker, or literally 'drained' of energy. Some people can be a drainer sometimes and an energizer at other times.

Exercise: Developing Your Relationship Map and Top Five Actions

Take a piece of blank paper or a fresh page in your journal and quickly scribble lots of circles across it. In each circle, write the name of someone you know. Start with people closest to you. You can include people you see regularly like your spouse/partner, children, friends, relatives, or even your hairdresser, therapist, gym coach, beautician, people on committees you participate in, work colleagues, bosses, neighbours, etc.

Once you've included as many people as seem relevant to the functioning of your life, take a coloured pen, say green, and circle all the energisers. In a different coloured pen, maybe red, circle all the drainers. If someone is particularly draining, you can make the line of the circle really thick.

Some people may not be either drainers or energisers. Leave them uncoloured. Some may be both energisers and drainers – mark them with both colours.

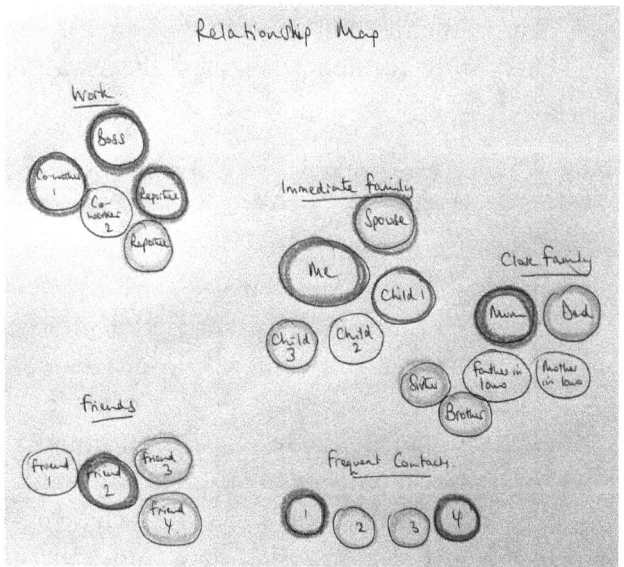

Figure 4: Relationship Map

In Figure 4 we've presented a template for illustration purposes. This imaginary person has three children one of whom is draining. The person's spouse is both an energiser and a drainer. They have a tricky work situation with three of their five closest work colleagues being a draining influence, as well as several other family, friends or frequent contacts. They have also circled themselves as a major drainer on themselves. Perhaps they realise they are particularly negative towards themself.

They also have a number of energisers in their life; one of their children, their spouse, several of their close family and a couple of friends and frequent contacts.

Now look at your relationship map and answer the following questions:

- Is your map predominantly green for energisers or red for drainers?
- Are the people you see most frequently or who have a big influence on your life energizers or drainers?

Drainers

- Can you minimise the time you spend with drainers? For instance, if you have a parent who is very draining, who perhaps ridicules or puts you down, can you reduce the time you see them?
- Can you eliminate the people who are drainers from your life? Do you have a friend who is always burdening you with their woes and troubles, but is indifferent about your challenges and just seems to take, take, take from you? Is this person really a friend? Can you let them go as a friend and make space to spend more time with people who energise you?
- Can you confront the drainers with how they make you feel and provide feedback so their

behaviour changes, transforming them into energisers? For instance, if there is someone at work who drains you, can you provide feedback to them or through their line manager, to improve their behaviour? Alternatively, can you change departments or jobs?

- Is your partner draining or energising you? If they are draining you, can you discuss with them how to bring more energising times together into your lives? For instance, do you go on date nights? Do you still make love? If not, identify clear actions to bring you and your partner closer together, including who will look after your children at these times. Even if you create energising times only once or twice per year, it is essential for a healthy relationship, your own energy levels and, therefore, your children's well-being.
- Do you sometimes find your children draining? Full-time parents or parents of a disabled child need to ensure they protect their energy from the demands of parenting. This is not a failure or doing your child a disservice; it's a reality. The emotional ups and downs of having a disabled child rarely go away. There may be periods of time when things are better – but they can also get worse. It can be physically, mentally and emotionally draining to deal with the worry, fear, lack of sleep and pain at seeing your child suffer – not to mention the mental juggling act of caring for your child, other children and working (especially if you are a consultant or don't have extended leaves of parenting time). If you don't take time to energise yourself, you are doing

your children a disservice, as well as yourself and your partner.

Energisers

- Who are your energisers? Do you have enough of them?
- Can you spend more time with them, or increase the number of energisers in your life? Perhaps you could join clubs or committees where you meet new people, or invite out a mum or parent of one of your children's friends whom you like a lot.
- How could you energise yourself further? What activities could you introduce into your life to counteract the drainers and just generally energise you? For instance, I started working out at the gym, ninjutsu, and tennis. Learning new things energises me and makes me feel good, physically and mentally. I treat myself to a beauty treatment every six weeks. I also find reflexology (therapeutic foot massage) heavenly, so I treat myself and Saafi to that sometimes. It is nourishing to my body and a great preventative health treatment.

If you have few or no drainers in your life – good for you! That's brilliant.

If your drainers are manageable, there is still room for more energisers to counterbalance them.

If you have major drainers close to you, this is where you really need to watch your energy levels, take major counteractive action and, if possible, minimise the time with these drainers or eliminate them from your life.

Now reflect on your answers to this exercise. Take five minutes to write down as many things as you can think of, to bring more energisers into your life and release drainers from your life. Time yourself.

Identify five priority actions related to the energisers and drainers in this section, and commit to doing these actions in the next four weeks. Hold yourself accountable for undertaking these actions.

Letting Go of a Draining Relationship

The nature and closeness of your relationship to a drainer dictates how possible it will be to let them go. The first step in terms of letting go of a draining relationship is identifying what is in your best interest and highest good, and that of your children. For me, it took many years to realise that my husband, whom I loved, was not only draining but damaging me. When I realised my children were also suffering by living in a toxic emotional maelstrom, that is when I gained the strength to leave; but it took a further two years to ensure a smooth exit that was easy on the children.

The following visualisation is one of my favourites. You may have come across it on my website. I find it invaluable to help me make decisions. I use it for all types of decisions, big and small.

In this visualisation, you access your highest guidance and/or deepest intuition. Each option is represented by a gate and through the gate you see, feel and experience the result of that choice. For instance, one gate could represent leaving your husband or wife, another could represent staying, and another could represent taking time out from the relationship without the drastic step of separation or divorce.

How does each choice feel? Sometimes I find a vial of eternal life on a golden gate with multi-coloured swirls. When I step through the gate, it is an amazing fanfare with all my loved ones celebrating amid lush vegetation, with an idyllic waterfall and natural swimming pool, swaying trees, and vibrant flowers beneath a blue sun-kissed sky.

If it is a choice I shouldn't take, sometimes the gate is black and oily and stacked high with massive grey boulders, so I can't even open it.

For any difficult decision, however big or small, the following visualisation always provides me with additional and sometimes decisive insight:

Visualisation to Help with Difficult Decisions

- **Sit on a chair with your feet firmly on the floor**, your arms unfolded and your hands resting on your thighs, palms up. Close your eyes. Ask for your best and highest guidance in this meditation, to help you make the best and highest choice with respect to your decision at hand.
- **Relax your body.** Become aware of your breathing. Imagine beautiful golden roots growing out of the soles of your feet, burrowing deep into the soil, welding you to the Earth.
- **Imagine Archangel Michael standing behind you.** Ask him to place his heavy blue cloak of protection upon your shoulders, to zip it up from beneath your feet to your chin, and to place the hood over your upper chakras so your whole mind, body and aura are completely protected.
- **With each breath you become more relaxed and heavy.** Your breathing becomes slower and deeper.

- **Imagine you are standing on a path in the countryside.** On each side of the path are gates. There is one gate for each choice you have regarding the important decision in your mind. There may be two choices, or three, or even four.
- **You walk up to the first gate.** This represents one of your choices. What does the gate look like? Is the gate smooth and polished, or does it have splinters and a rough finish? What colour is the gate? Does it seem inviting? Open the gate. Does it open easily or is it stiff?
- **Now step through into the space behind the gate.** What is there? Is it open countryside? Or beautiful garden and forests? Are there people there? Are they happy or sad? What is the weather like? Do you feel at peace – happy? Do you feel ill at ease, scared or alone? Feel free to explore further. Walk around, go as far as you wish, and when you have finished looking around, come back to the gate. Walk back through the gate and onto the path.
- **Now walk to the next gate.** This represents your next choice. What does the gate look like? What does it feel like? Do you want to enter?
- **Now open the gate and step through the gateway.** What do you see? What do you feel? Who do you see? Explore.
- **When you are ready, leave through the gate you entered** and step back onto the path.
- **For every choice, there is a gate.** Go to that gate and repeat the previous steps. What does each gate look and feel like? Open them one by one, step inside and look around. Explore. What do you see and feel?

- **When you have explored the space behind every gate, come back to the centre of the pathway**. When you are ready, wiggle your toes, shrug your shoulders and open your eyes. You have now left the meditation.

Interpreting the Visualisation

When I do this meditation, it is always starkly obviously which choice will lead to the best outcome for me. Within the same meditation, inside one gate may be a barren wasteland, freezing, with rain and storms and rocks, and I'm alone. In contrast, through another gateway there may be an abundance of colourful flowers, emerald trees, happy people laughing and partying, waterfalls, sunlight and birdsong. The choice you should take is the place behind the gates that makes you feel most radiant.

Sometimes two choices have a similar feel to them. In this case, either choice is fine to take. If no gateway reveals a place you'd like to stay, then consider another choice you haven't yet explored. There is always a gateway that will reveal a positive place. You may need to search for it along the path. Ask what choice this gateway represents.

It's important to state your intention at the beginning, e.g. 'Dear Source/my Guardian Angel, please guide me for my best and highest path in this decision', or similar words and intention. Whether you ask Source or your Guardian Angel, you will get the same result, as angels communicate the word of Source. This means you will be guided by Source or your Guardian Angel to receive the recommendations within the meditation aligned with your highest path.

Even if you don't specify guidance from Source or your Guardian Angel but just ask for your highest guidance in this meditation, it will work. It is a great way to access your deepest, truest intuition on this decision.

✦Visualisation: Letting Go of a Draining Relationship, with the Help of Archangel Michael✦

Feel your feet on the earth. Imagine beautiful golden roots growing out of the soles of your feet. Become aware of your breathing.

Imagine a ball of white light at the base of your feet. As you breathe in, the light fills your calves, thighs, torso, arms, neck, and head. When you exhale, breathe out multi-coloured stars from the crown of your head, taking away all the stresses and strains of the day. With each breath, you relax more and more, sinking towards the ground.

Ask Archangel Michael to place his blue cloak of protection around your shoulders and zip it up from beneath your feet to your chin. He pulls the hood over your upper chakras, so you are completely protected.

Now imagine you are in a wide valley. The grass is green, but it is night-time. The moon is full and you are bathed in beams of silver light. In front of you appears the person you wish to release from your life. Standing opposite you, the person is smiling and you realise this is the highest self of the person you wish to release. This is their soul. It is good and understands why you wish to release them.

If you feel like it, explain why you want to release the person from your life. Explain that it is time to move on – for both of you. Make it clear you wish the person well.

Archangel Michael appears beside you. His blue wings are amazing. He is large and strong and invincible. He specialises in protection, but also in cutting the unhealthy cords that bind you to relationships you no longer need.

Now you see that you are connected to the person you wish to release from your life by millions of tiny blue energy lines. They go from your body to the body of the person you wish to release. Some are thicker than others. Archangel Michael takes his sword. He is going to cut through these energy lines.

As he brings down his sword, he severs these energy lines easily, and they fall apart and disappear completely. You now stand whole, disconnected, and healed.

Thank the soul of the person you wish to leave. Thank Archangel Michael. When you are ready, come back to the room more able to move on.

Note: This is a great meditation, but leaving can be a difficult process, depending on the nature of your relationship. Leaving a marriage is particularly challenging. This visualisation can be used numerous times.

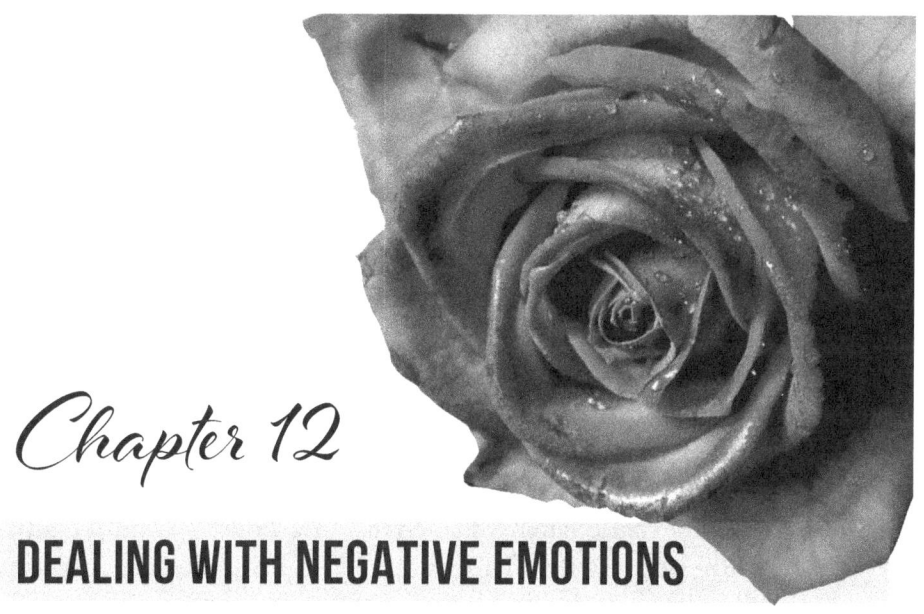

Chapter 12
DEALING WITH NEGATIVE EMOTIONS

Negative emotions are not a sign of failure: they are part of our journey to enlightenment. Negative emotions like fear, anger and guilt are commonly felt when we have any traumatic or earth-shaking experience. These emotions are commonly experienced when we have a disabled child. We must embrace them, congratulate ourselves on how good we are at these negative emotions (as this in itself helps shake up the energies, making them easier to release) and work at turning them into positives.

This section explains what negative emotions look like at an energetic level and how damaging they can be to our health and the health of others. Then, we provide specific visualisations for calling in celestial beings to help us turn these emotions into positives.

Energetic Defence Mechanisms

When, at a soul level, we choose to enter Earth we agree to accept the Veil of Amnesia that sets Earth apart from most other worlds. In doing this, we forget that we are connected to Source, that most of us have had many previous incarnations, and that we will always be supported, protected, loved, nourished – if only we believe in the flow of abundance.

This is why there is a queue of souls trying to get a place in Earth – there just aren't many training grounds like it. To wrestle with the ego – to deal with the physical and sexual challenges of living in a body – is unlike any other experience. Unfortunately fear and anxiety are one of the main challenges that we, as humans, must overcome to reunite ourselves with Source and merge with our soul/higher self.

Our ego is intrinsically insecure and sets up defence mechanisms to deal with its fear. These defence mechanisms manifest in two main ways:

1) Guarding around the body, like armour that blocks the flow of energy through the body and the balance of the chakras. This often manifests in particular body shapes.
2) Unhealthy energetic behaviours.

The following diagrams illustrate how these emotions look at an energetic level. You can imagine how harmful they can be, both to you and when directed towards others.

In illustration A, the person on the left uses the person on the right as a one-way source of energy. The person on the left is an energy drainer. Depression can be linked to this illustration, although people can drain others' energy without being depressed.

In illustration B the person is prickly and irritable, being an emotional porcupine. Guilt can be illustrated by illustration C, where energetic weapons are turned inwards, to punish yourself. Anger is an emotion easily associated with illustration D, hysteria combined with sending emotional darts that hurt the other person.

Be aware of negative energy patterns that you may be using. Do your best to neutralise them or turn them into positive energy patterns. The tools and strategies outlined in this book will help you with this.

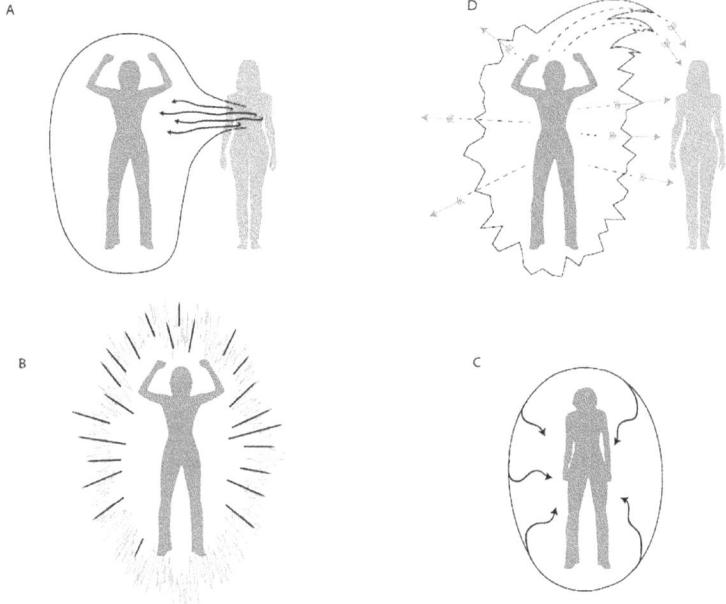

Figure 5: Negative energetic behaviours

A: Energy sucking from the solar plexus; emotional leech
B: Porcupine – stay away or else
C: Self-loathing, brooding, attacking oneself
D: Hysteria combined with mental darts fired at others

Guilt, Fear and Anger

Guilt is like toxic sludge sitting in our bodies. It does harm to us – remember the water theory and how thoughts affect our bodies and health? Guilt contaminates our bodies and can lead to disease. We need to deal with it and continue to manage it.

With a disabled child, the drivers of guilt can take many forms. As mothers, we can feel guilty for something we did or didn't do during pregnancy or labour that contributed to our child becoming disabled. This may or may not be based on medical evidence.

As fathers, we may feel guilty for not being as supportive as we could have been during pregnancy, or birth, or for decisions taken that may or may not have contributed to the disability. I've known fathers who feel guilty for it being their sperm that fertilised the egg.

We can feel guilty for not spending enough time with our children, for resenting the time spent with our children, for resenting our child's disability. We may feel guilty for being angry or sad at the life we lost, or thought we were going to have. We could feel guilty for being short-tempered with our children or spouse or other people – for not honouring ourselves – for being less than we thought we could be – for being what we see as imperfect in any one of a million-plus ways.

The first step to minimising guilt is understanding the drivers of guilt. What do you feel you guilty about? These can be big things or small things, or sometimes seemingly minute things. They can be things in the past or things in the future. Note them all down in a quick five-minute brain dump.

Exercise: Identifying Guilt

> Have your journal and a pen or pencil ready. Take five minutes to brain dump what you feel guilty about. Be honest and don't judge yourself.

Spiritually, it is important to recognise that some things we feel guilty about may stem from previous life experiences or ancestral programming (several generations of our ancestors' beliefs and feelings have been neurologically found to be imprinted on our brains, requiring deep, consistent re-programming to correct). Here we will focus on conscious current life guilt.

For best results, this next visualisation should be repeated regularly, together with the Forgiveness Creed (provided earlier).

✵Visualisation to Release Guilt with Archangel Chamuel✵

Close your eyes. Feel your feet on the floor and imagine tiny golden roots growing out of the soles of your feet.

Become aware of your breathing. Continue breathing slowly and evenly. Relax deeply. Ask Archangel Michael to put his blue cloak of protection around your shoulders, to zip it up from beneath your feet to your chin and pull the hood over your higher chakras. Know you are completely protected.

Imagine you are on a sandy beach next to a beautiful expanse of clear blue water. Your feet are bare and you can feel the sand soft and silky between your toes. You glance down and see that you are naked except for a bathing costume. You are completely alone and safe in the knowledge that no one will disturb you.

In the distance, a shining light glides over the surface of the alluring water. The sun is hot on your skin and although you know you won't burn, you find the look of the water enticing. As the light progresses towards you, you see that it is a beautiful angel, with wide open golden wings. It is the Archangel Chamuel, who works with self-love. She explains that guilt is a lack of self-love. We are angry at ourselves for being imperfect, yet our imperfections are perfect for our current situation. They give us the opportunity to learn, grow and become better people.

Take a moment to explain what you are feeling guilty about, and listen to her response.

From her gown, Chamuel withdraws a scroll of parchment. On this scroll is written the highest path you should take with respect to shifting the guilt you have acquired. It may be necessary to modify your behaviour, to do the same as you have been doing but be easier on yourself, or to do something more specific. It may be that what you are feeling guilty about was a one-off event never to be repeated – but it is still important to release the guilt. Read what is written on the scroll to see what is right for you.

Give Archangel Chamuel back the scroll. She explains that the sea before you is the Sea of Forgiveness. It is a wonderful, nurturing sea and washes away the guilt that is toxifying your body. It may be that the behaviour that has caused the guilt is not your fault, is not bad at all, or was not good behaviour and should not be repeated. Whatever the action, this sea will help you wash away the guilt, enabling you to be a freer, more whole being, allowing you to dedicate your life to being your highest self and walking your highest path, your path of highest potential.

When you are ready, walk into the sea and, in your own time, completely submerge yourself.

As you walk deeper into the sea, you feel each cell in your body become lighter and more energised. You feel your body actually light up as guilt is replaced by forgiveness and self-love. You feel the love of this Sea of Forgiveness. In this sea you are wholly loved and forgiven. Finally, allow your lungs to breathe in the water. Instead of filling your lungs with water, you are filled with love. This is a place you can come back to whenever you want to.

When you are ready, feel yourself rising from the sea so you hover above it. Thank Archangel Chamuel and, in your own time, return to the room.

Visualisation to Let Go of Anger

Ground and protect yourself.

Imagine you are lying on a cloud. It is soft and fluffy beneath you like a deep, nurturing quilt. Beside you is a small child angel, a cherub. He or she is giggling and delighted by playing a game - pouring a shining liquid from one golden goblet to another.

Each time the liquid passes between goblets, it changes colour. It starts red and ends pink-gold. It looks like a heavenly liquid, a liquid of the celestial kingdom.

The little cherub explains that when you first drink the red liquid, it brings all your anger to the surface of your body and mind. This is important because suppressed anger is dangerous to your health. If you keep anger trapped inside, it can lead to disease.

The cherub explains that when you drink from the other goblet, it frees the angry thoughts and feelings from your body, leaving you calm, peaceful and healthy.

You agree to drink from both goblets. First you drink from the goblet with the red liquid. It is sweet and delightful. It trickles down your throat refreshingly. You can feel it fill your stomach, and the fresh sensation flows through the whole of your body.

Now you become aware of angry thoughts floating to the surface of your mind. These thoughts can be about anything – about your children, spouse, work colleagues or boss – people you know, people you feel have wronged you or people you have wronged. Be aware of what the strongest thoughts and feelings are. Who are they directed against? Don't try to hold onto them; just let them bubble up. Continue to breathe deeply and easily.

The thoughts make you feel restless and irritated. The cherub passes you the other goblet, and you drink from it thirstily. The liquid is never-ending, so drink as much as you need to. Immediately the restlessness you felt begins to subside. The sweet calming taste of the liquid flows quickly throughout your body.

Answers may come to you about the root cause of those angry thoughts and actions against or involving you. Were you being taught a spiritual lesson? What were you meant to learn? Just be aware; don't judge yourself or others, for these are lessons you've been given to become a stronger, braver, more whole individual. The people who have made you angry are your best teachers.

If you have made yourself angry, what should you learn from yourself? What should you forgive yourself and others?

When you are ready, thank the cherub, return the goblets, and come back to the room. Roll your shoulders, rub your fingers and thumbs, and open your eyes.

Visualisation to Release Fear with Ray o' Light

I work with Ray o' Light regularly in all sorts of situations, when I feel fearful. Ray o' Light isn't of human ancestry, nor is he an angel. He is one of countless types of celestial beings that are beyond our human vocabulary. Whilst he doesn't have a gender as we understand him, I tend to experience his energy as male.

Get into position for meditation. Sit or lie down, with your arms and legs uncrossed, eyes closed and back straight. Become aware of your breathing. Ground and protect yourself.

When you are ready, imagine a golden warrior stands before you. He gleams with the most amazing golden amour. He wields a sparkling sword, a golden shield and gleaming helmet. Even his body leather is gold. The skin of his hands and what you can see of his face are also gold. The only colour on his body apart from gold is a brilliant ruby red gemstone embedded in a thick gold ring on the third finger of his right hand. This is Ray o' Light. He is beyond powerful and he works with all beings on their fearlessness – when fear is a useless factor. Know that he will never make you fearless when fear keeps you protected.

Now ask him the following questions:

- How can you make me fearless?
- How can I help myself to be fearless?

Listen to his response.

Now Ray o' Light is going to become your armour. He is going to stand within you. This is possible, as he is energetic rather than physically bodied.

He stands within you now. His energetic form is bigger than you. He completely encloses your energetic and physical body in his powerful armour and fearlessness.

Take a few moments to become aware of the energies settling in you and how they make you feel. At any point you can ask him to leave, but by allowing him to stand within you, you take on some of his powerful energy. This can help you in your life journey and challenges.

When you are ready, become aware of your feet on the ground, roll your shoulders, gently move your head, and open your eyes. Feel the strength of Ray o' Light within you, as you continue your day.

Chapter 13

CREATING HOPE THROUGH NEW TECHNOLOGIES

The speed of technological development is phenomenal. I recently spoke with an ex-colleague of mine who has a teenage son with severe cerebral palsy. His son is unable to speak and is in a wheelchair, but with the small amount of control he has in his right hand, he is able to use an iPad to communicate. The iPad speaks for him. He has numerous friends similarly challenged, has a busy social life, he recently gave a speech at his father's birthday and he is going to college. He is living a full and vibrant life.

Eye computers, mobility aids and advanced teaching techniques (when available) can transform a young person's life and those of their caregivers. New stem cell technology provides additional hope that within a generation, the lives of our beloved children will be easier.

In South Africa, there isn't the free support that comes with living in Britain, but we are still far more fortunate than in most African countries where there is negligible support for disabled children and their families from the state, and limited private or charitable care. It is one of my dreams to bring advanced therapy schools to Africa.

In the following visualisation, I ask you to step up to being a Light-worker for the planet. This is someone who spiritually prays or meditates for more than just benefit to themselves, but to wider communities and ultimately the planet. The important thing to understand about angels is that they are most active when asked to help. In this visualisation, we ask the Ascended Master Leonardo da Vinci to help give new technology and wisdom to the Earth to help benefit children like ours.

Visualisation to Bring New Technologies into Your Life

Feel your feet on the floor. Become aware of your breathing. Breathe in and out, in and out. Breathe evenly and deeply. Imagine a ball of white light surrounding you, protecting and cleansing you. Ask for this meditation to help you realise your best and highest potential and the best and highest potential of the world.

Find yourself floating in space. Around you, rather than blackness, space dazzles with brilliant shining stars and planets. You can see the Earth millions of miles from you, a gleaming sphere of blue and green just like in the space documentaries you have viewed.

Beside you hovers a dazzling human. This person is vaguely familiar to you. You realise it is Leonardo da Vinci, the famous painter, inventor and genius who lived centuries ago. He is one of many historical figures revered for his innovation and range and depth of interests, from anatomy, to engineering, physics to palaeontology, art and sculpture. He painted the *Mona Lisa*. He is an Ascended

Master and works in the celestial kingdom to bring new information and wisdom to the planet Earth.

'I am here to help bring down new technologies that will benefit you and your disabled child', he says.

You ask him what you have to do to help bring these technologies through. He may have specific advice for you. Listen to what he says.

He takes your hand and helps you fly towards a glittering planet that is near to Earth but a golden purple colour, rather than green and blue. As you enter the atmosphere of this strange planet, you feel a rush of knowledge and power malleable for the good of the world and universe.

Around you, glowing humans fly gracefully. They smile at you as you pass. The world you have entered seems to gleam with health and abundance. Families play games together, something similar to chess, boules and other strange games that take place in the air among the people playing, with unusual pieces that look like fairies and dragons.

You see a young boy bring his hands together and a bowl of delicious steaming porridge materialises in his palms. There are simple buildings that, when you look in, are luxurious for sitting, lying and reading. Athletes stretch and laugh with each other as they seek to outrun or out-jump one another. Everyone seems happy, healthy and content.

'This is the highest potential of the Earth', says Leonardo. 'In this world everyone is healed and healthy. On Earth the wisest souls have come back as disabled children, or children with terminal diseases. It is a tough and stretching life lesson. As humans become ready for new wisdom, technology will become available to make life for disabled children and adults easier. This will provide many new lessons for the disabled children, but in particular for others around them. Souls of disabled children and adults have agreed to more difficult life paths in order to give others around them stretching lessons, as well as to hone their own soul lessons.

'Are you ready to take new wisdom to Earth? We can only give new technologies and wisdom if humans ask for it. Ask for information and it will flow to the right people and organisations on the planet Earth. By doing this, you become a Light-worker, someone bringing light to the planet Earth'.

If you are ready to ask for help for the world, do so now and receive whatever Leonardo gifts you. It could be pure light; it could be a feeling or sensation; it could be a symbol or an object, even a book. Receive whatever he passes to you. Thank him and, when you are ready, allow yourself to be transported back to the planet Earth and the room and place you are meditating in.

In your own time, feel your feet on the ground, roll your shoulders and open your eyes.

Chapter 14

SETTING GOALS

This is a really empowering chapter. Being spiritual is about both visualising what you want and manifesting it in the earthly plane. Manifestation doesn't occur by just sitting cross-legged meditating. Manifestation requires taking action in the physical plane, <u>*doing*</u> stuff that can bring about what you want to happen.

I've found the best way to bring things about is to set clear goals, with clear target dates. This declutters the mind and gives it something to aim for.

In this section, you will identify your goals by accessing both your conscious mind and your subconscious and highest guidance. I then describe how you can formulate teams of people to help you realise the goals you have determined.

Honing In on Your Goals

The diagram below illustrates how goal time frames can be broken down. Whilst we are going to focus on identifying one-year, five-year, ten-year and lifetime goals, in your own time you can also start to identify daily, weekly and monthly goals to help you achieve your longer-term aims.

Exercise: Use Your Conscious Mind to Identify Your Goals

Don't overthink this exercise. In just ten minutes, brain dump all the goals you'd like to achieve in your life, including the wildest goals you may have hidden deep down.

The key is to think out of the box – think big and allow your imagination to flow.

Exercise: Channelling Your Goals

In this exercise, you access your 'highest guidance'. This might be guidance from your Guardian Angel, a wise Ascended Master, God/Source, or your soul. For this, we are going to draw on the tool of 'channelling' or 'trans-writing'.

Channelling is fun, and it gets easier with practice. Whether you believe you are accessing your highest guidance or your deepest intuition, doesn't matter. What is important is that you relax your mind, let your ego step out of the picture, and allow whatever messages and insights arise to flow through your pen or from your keyboard onto your computer screen.

- Sit in a chair at a table or anywhere you can comfortably write/type.
- Look at the following diagram, keeping in mind the intention of identifying your one-year, five-

year and ten-year goals. Also keep in mind the areas of your life that we've discussed earlier, in the heart of wellbeing.

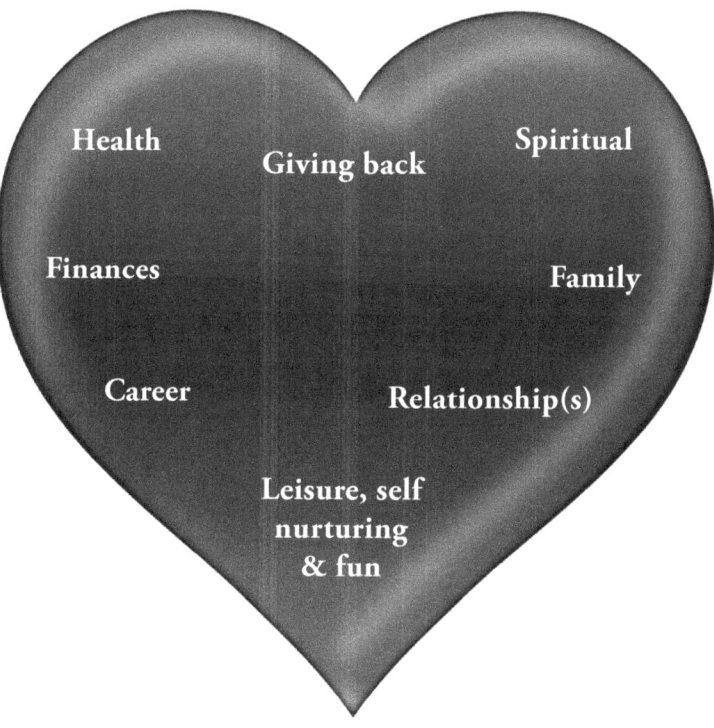

- Place your journal and pen, or your computer (if you prefer to type, like I do) in front of you.
- Close your eyes. Place your feet flat on the floor – or if you are sitting cross-legged, try to keep your back relatively straight.
- Become aware of your breathing. Breathe in and out, in and out. Slow your breathing as you would when you go into meditation.
- Ground and protect yourself.

- Ask Archangel Gabriel to pour white light of purification through your mind, body and aura. Feel this beautiful cleansing process lighten your body. Continue to feel this white light surround and sink into every pore and cell in your body.
- Ask for your highest guidance to give you insight into your life and your goals. Then, just allow a free flow of information to run through your pen or fingers. Don't worry about getting the spelling right or keeping things neat. Just allow the information to flow without controlling it. Don't censor what comes through; there is no right or wrong. Write and type until there are no more ideas left to come through.
- When you have exhausted the information, ask if there is any other highest guidance that is important for you to receive at the moment. This may have to do with priorities, what you need to do immediately, or how you might do something.
- Thank your highest guidance for being available to you.
- When you are ready, become aware of your body, feel your feet on the ground, roll your ankles, shrug your shoulders and open your eyes.

These next steps can be done now or saved for later:

- Read through what you've written or typed. If you want, correct some of the spelling – I always make a lot of typos when I touch-type with my eyes closed.
- See what information has come through. Is it surprising? Can you organise it at all into imme-

diate priority goals, one-year goals, five-year goals or longer-term aims?
- Do you have a clearer idea of what your heart and your wisest guidance want for you in this life?
- On a separate page, write in big letters at the top 'MY GOALS'. Structure these into time frames, e.g. over one year, over five years, ten years, life goals, etc.
- Which are the most important to you? Circle these and put a target date for when you wish to achieve them.
- Are there any immediate steps you can jot down to help you reach these goals? Now you are starting to form your action plan.

Goal Helpers & Goal Teams

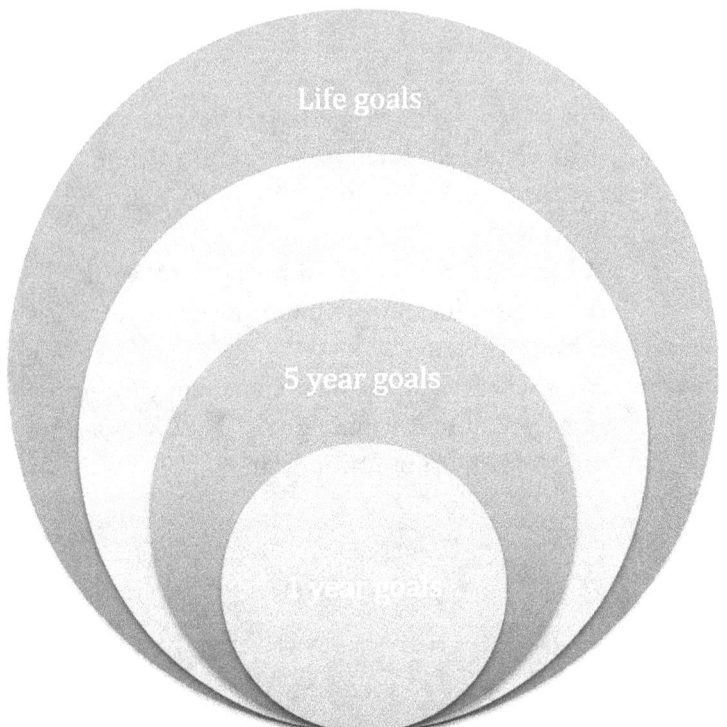

Figure 6: Goal Map

Return to the goals you set for one year, five years and longer. Now choose one goal you want to achieve this year.

Take your relationship map and see who can help you get there. Label this person 'Goal Helper' and circle the name in a new colour.

What is a Goal Helper? Just that – someone who can help you achieve your goal. It's not a formal title. You don't even need to tell them they're on your Goal Team. But it helps to know you have a support base and who is in that support base. If the team seems insufficient, you know you have to seek out other people who can help you.

For instance, perhaps your goal is excellent health and strength within the year, to be able to lift your disabled child without hurting your back. This would require working out at the gym or doing a Pilates class. Who can help you achieve this goal? Would it include a sister or partner to help look after your children when you are at your class? Is there someone who also wants to get fit and whom you like spending time with, whom you can buddy with?

Is there a specific goal you have for your child(ren)? Who can help you reach that goal? Maybe a teacher at school? A parents' support group, to swap health and therapy ideas with?

Maybe your goal is a new job. Who do you know that can help you explore new jobs, or who may be in an organisation you wish to join? Is there someone who can review your CV or give you career advice?

When I was between jobs earlier recently, I used it as an opportunity to reach out to old friends and colleagues I'd lost touch with. One of whom was an ex-boss. When I had worked with her, I called her my Fairy Godmother, because she always looked out for me and gave me wise and loving advice.

I updated her about my current situation – my contract ending, the divorce, my disabled child, etc. – and she offered to give me two days of life coaching. This was an amazing, pivotal opportunity that I accepted. My Fairy Godmother helped me talk through my hopes and dreams, and narrow them down to clear, defined goals that I could act on. These goals were about work, but also about relationships, children, and life in general.

I learned from a single mum friend of mine not to be afraid of asking. People don't mind being asked, and if they do, they can gracefully decline. I recommend getting a mentor for every goal you have. A health mentor can be a personal coach or a friend who has done what you need to do. A divorce mentor is a lawyer/solicitor. Don't be afraid to ask. People get energy from helping.

Here are some of my Goal Teams:

1) My children's happiness team – Saafi's caregivers, school teachers and therapists, and the ABR therapy support group for cerebral palsy, Tariq's school teacher and school secretary, my friends who have children in my children's classes (they know what's going on and can remind me if I forget), Saafi's paediatrician and neurologist, the support group for mums with CP children, Tariq's tennis coach and his friends' parents, my parents, my children's father.
2) My divorce team – my lawyer, advocate, friends and family who provide emotional support and advice.
3) My health and well-being team – my close friends and family, my integrated health physician, my kinesiologist, my reflexologist, my tennis coach, personal trainer, ninja sensei, physician, domestic and garden helpers.
4) Job team – my employer, my work team, my Fairy Godmother/mentor, network of professional colleagues, LinkedIn social media app, headhunters I've met through the course of my work, ex-employers, clients, friends who review my CV.

5) Fun team – my close girlfriends (sometimes I specifically ask them to help with certain activities – so, I have a friend I go to the spa with and also a cinema buddy).
6) Wealth team – my personal banker, a friend who knows about financial planning, lawyer, health insurance admin staff.
7) Author business – my publishing mentor, reviewers, proofreader, admin support, Insight Timer admin team.

Conclusion

BRINGING IT ALL TOGETHER

I want to give some suggestions in terms of bringing the spiritual practice, tools and exercises into your daily practice, and a checklist of what you should have completed in this book, which should form your Action Plan going forward.

Checklist

- ✓ Do you have a clear record of your goals (over one year, five years and longer) for each area of your life, e.g. spiritual/personal development, family, leisure/pleasure, financial, career, giving back, health?
- ✓ Which goals have you prioritized? Do you have at least one one-year goal in each area of your life? Write these down clearly.
- ✓ Have you listed three immediate actions you can take for each of these one-year goals? Have you put a target date on them for when you wish to complete them?

- ✓ Have you identified your goal teams/mentors to help you get there? Have at least one mentor for your overriding priority goal.
- ✓ If you've completed everything in this checklist – this is your Action Plan.

Incorporating spirituality into your daily life:

1) Ground and protect yourself every morning.
2) Every morning visualise a wonderful day ahead of you. Feel the sensation of this amazing day in every cell of your body.
3) Repeat a positive affirmation that you have chosen to work on for 30 days. It could have to do with money, self-worth, attracting your perfect career, health for your child, or fulfilment in some other way.
4) Last thing at night, give thanks to Source/God/the Universe for at least three things relating to the day.
5) Last thing at night, in bed, or in a quiet space during the day, undertake a visualisation to release a negative emotion.

The spiritual lessons I've learnt during the first five years of Saafi's life have been intense and I think have enabled a step-change in who I am as a person. Particularly challenging have been lessons to do with self-forgiveness, releasing guilt, and bouncing back from periods of high stress. Saafi and his brother Tariq have given me so much love and joy and magical moments. I feel blessed to have them both and I thank the universe for them, every single day. I also thank Source for the many lessons the experience of having Saafi has taught me, and for the constant support I get from the celestial kingdom.

So what does all this mean for understanding our children with disability?

1) Don't pity our children. Respect them for the powerful souls they are and admire them for the difficult paths they have chosen.
2) Explore the lessons they are here to teach you, through the visualisations in this book.
3) Explore whether your life purpose is connected with your child's disability.
4) If you are having difficulty communicating with your child, consider trying to communicate with them on the energetic plane (through psychic communication).
5) What light does it shed on the relationships with our other loved ones, e.g. spouse, children or other family members?
6) What do you need to do to thrive and prosper in this life?

If you look at these questions and take them into your spiritual pursuit, I believe you, like me, will find the platinum lining in the journey with our special children.

Be loving, be brave, be your highest self, a wonderful, amazing being. I wish you love, joy, success, and prosperity along the way.

Free Audio Meditation

To get your free guided meditation, go to:
http://LightseekersWay.com/SSDaudio

Connect On Social Media

Twitter: @HelenaClareLSW

Website: www.LightseekersWay.com

CONTACT HELENA
Contact Helena about speaking engagements, media appearances or just to say hello at
www.LightseekersWay.com

Appendix 1

ANGELS & DIVINE MESSAGES

Angels are messengers of God/Source or whatever you choose to call the universal consciousness that governs our world. It's often easier to communicate directly with angels than with God because they vibrate at a frequency closer to that of humans, albeit still much higher. They are celestial beings of unconditional love and goodness, and they are queuing up to help us on our best and highest paths, and to help the world become a better place within which to live.

Working with angels and Archangels and allowing them to support you on your journey with disability will be a massive power source in difficult times, to help you achieve your greatest and most sacred goals. Working with these amazing beings of light is fascinating, exciting and turbocharging!

A few other things to know about angels…

They are not the intellectual property of any single religion.

Many religions talk about angels, but that does not make them Christian or Muslim or the property of any other religion that claims them. There is one truth and humans have different paths of accessing that truth. All are fine as long as they're followed with the intention of light and love.

Angels do not have a gender as humans know gender.

They are not women or men, just like God is not a woman or a man, but they do form themselves in the image of men or women. They may come to you in a beautiful female form, or a strong warrior male or clown or child. Whatever image they present to you, just accept it.

Angels don't have ego.

One of the things that makes us earthly is that we have 'ego' manifesting in insecurities, fears, bravado, and so on. Angels are beings of pure unconditional love. They don't judge us. They love us unconditionally – how cool is that!

Angels also don't have free will.

They are extensions of the Source Energy, or God.

How are divine messages received?

People receive divine messages in four main ways. Some people are **clairvoyant**: they see pictures in their minds or see spirits around them. Other people are **claircognisant**: they just *know* the divine message (often called gut instinct or intuition). Other people feel angels or energies around them or experience a physical sensation: they are known as **clairsentient.**

I am **clairaudient**; I hear voices of the angels, and other celestial beings, as clearly as a person standing right beside me. For almost 30 years they've given me constant guidance and support and sometimes breath-stopping insight and prediction. Angels will never interfere with a person's own free will except when a person's life is threatened and it is not yet their time to die. You have to *ask* to have your request supported.

What is so special about a Guardian Angel?

Everyone in the world has a unique Guardian Angel who works only with that person during every incarnation they experience. That means on your first incarnation on Earth they were watching over you and only you, and in your last incarnation they will still be watching over you and only you. This is such a special relationship, which is why your Guardian Angel is the first angel I will teach you to connect with.

> *We are here for you. Just ask us to help. We never judge, we only love, whoever you are.*
> *– Azekial (Helena's Guardian Angel)*

What are the Archangels?

Archangels such as Gabriel or Michael are leaders of groups of angels and specialise in particular forms of support. They are ready to assist you when you ask them. Time in the angelic world is not the same as on the earthly plane, so don't underestimate how powerful the angels are.

Never think you are unworthy of their time. They have infinite time to help you on your highest path, if you ask for their help to help the world.

What are Ascended Masters?

Ascended Masters are highly evolved beings along the human evolution chain. They are great leaders such as Jesus, Mother Mary, the Prophet Mohammed, the Buddha, Ghandi, Nelson Mandela, Pallas Athena, Kuan Yin, Mary Magdalene and Lady Portia. If you have devoted your life in some way to helping others or the planet, Ascended Masters are there to work with you to increase your impact. Ascended Masters are both male and female, and from all races and ages in history.

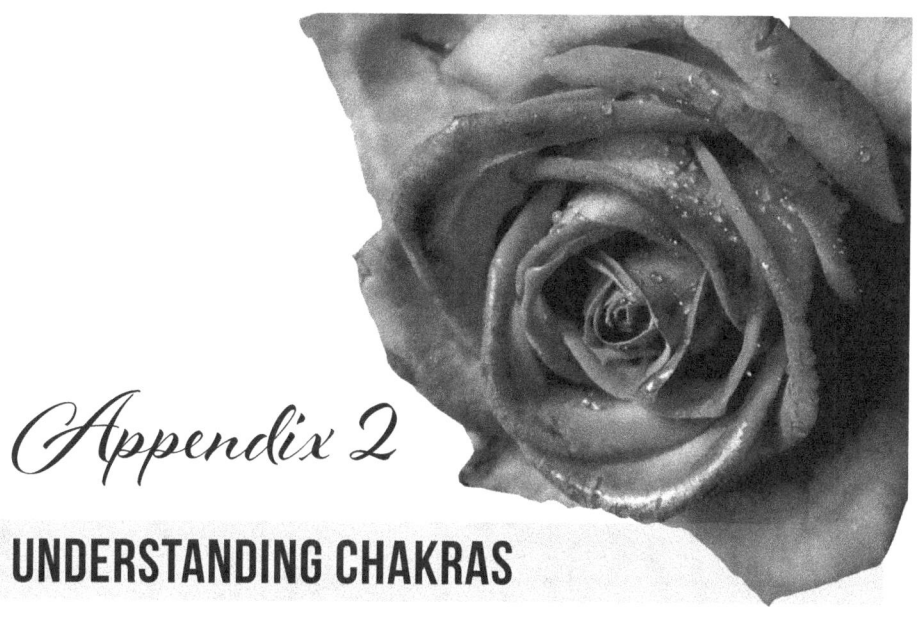

Appendix 2

UNDERSTANDING CHAKRAS

Chakra is a Sanskrit world meaning 'wheel' or 'disc'. Chakras are energy centres within our body, the points of maximum energy intake. If our chakras are out of balance, our whole energy field is out of balance.

Each chakra links to a particular layer of our aura, also known as our light body. They also link to specific body parts, emotions and issues. In many books you'll find seven chakras presented within the body. These are, in ascending order from the lowest, at the base of the spine;

- the root or base chakra
- the sacral
- the solar plexus
- the heart
- the throat
- the third eye
- the crown

For maximum impact, I work with nine chakras. The extra two are important. The earth or earth star chakra is located beneath your feet, in the earth. It stimulates your life potential. The star chakra is above your head and provides a stronger link with the Divine.

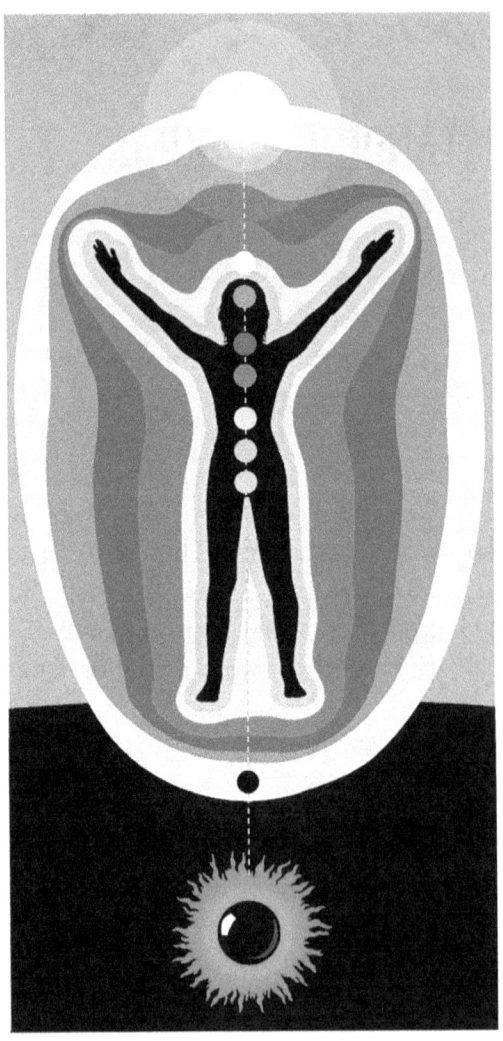

Figure 5: The Nine Chakras

To experiment with measuring your chakras, lie down on your back and hold a pendulum above the point of the chakra you want to focus on, about 30 cm away from the body. Allow the movement of the chakra to pull the pendulum in a particular direction or shape.

If there is no movement at all, this means the chakra is blocked or the energy coming from it is stagnant. If the chakra spins clockwise, this generally suggests the chakra is open and healthy. If it spins anti-clockwise, there are likely to be negative associations with that chakra. These can be understood by considering the significance of that chakra. For instance, a strongly anti-clockwise spin in the sacral chakra could suggest issues relating to sexuality or a lack of creativity. If this continues over a long period of time, it could lead to physical problems in the prostate/bladder or lower-back issues, or even frigidity and impotence.

For a full chakra analysis of the meaning behind different chakra oscillations, I've found Barbara Ann Brennan's *Hands of Light* to be outstanding. Barbara can see auras and chakras and disease manifesting in the aura before reaching the physical body.

By cleansing and energising the chakras, physical conditions can be avoided. If they do manifest, one possible reason is that issues relating to that chakra have not been dealt with adequately. This is why we need to recognise the energetic nature of ourselves, rather than concentrating merely on the physical. I've listed on my website some of the amazing books that have helped me.

Additionally, Louise Hay has developed a set of affirmations that, if repeated on a regular basis, can cause a shift in mindset at the auric level, healing disease in the physical body. When you have a complaint or illness, it is useful to check Louise Hay's list to see if the associated issue resonates; if it does, work on the auric level through affirmations and visualisations, as well as employing physical remedies (which often only address the symptoms).

My own channelled book *Velocity Ascension* is a training manual on how to become a Light-worker. It also includes a list of ailments and how to remedy them, which Archangels to work with on specific health challenges, and how to cleanse and heal your chakras and aura to improve your health, well-being and ability to contribute to the world's ascension, as well as ascend yourself.

How Chakras Relate to Our Spiritual Path

Archangels are assigned to specific chakras. By working with them we can increase the pace of our healing and spiritual enlightenment. Our spiritual aim on Earth is to reach enlightenment, also known as *Ascension*; this is where we are wise enough and good enough to join the ranks of the Ascended Masters: men and women such as Mother Mary, Pallas Athena, Prophet Mohammed, Buddha, Jesus, all of whom have reached the same level of vibration as angels - the **seventh dimension.**

Most people in the world currently are in the **third dimension**; they are driven by materialism, greed, dogmatism, fear and survival. When you reach the **fourth dimension** you have gained a strong sense of the importance of caring for others, treating others how you would like to be treated yourself, a recognition that there may be something more important than material wealth, and an initial step along your *spiritual* journey. This is different from a *religious* path, where one could be senior in the hierarchy of a religion but remain in the third dimension because of a belief that only your way is right and others are wrong – judgement is not spiritual and holds back one's spiritual growth.

In the **fifth dimension** a person has made strides along their spiritual journey and connected to their 'soul' or higher self. They actively aspire to be their higher self, and to be on their best and highest path.

In the **sixth dimension** a person has become a junior Ascended Master. They still have lessons to accomplish but are active Light-workers, committing themselves in some way to the best and highest good of the planet, contributing to raising the planet's vibrations, and they will demonstrate traits of unconditional love, strength, integrity, joy and abundance. Princess Diana was a junior Ascended Master.

As a person progresses through each dimension, the colour of the chakra changes and the fundamental aspect of the person as they relate to that chakra progresses. For example, for the heart chakra a person will move from the affirmation 'I AM Touch' in the third dimension to:

- 'I AM Feelings' in the fourth dimension
- 'I AM Unconditional Love' in the fifth dimension
- 'I AM the Heart of the Universe' in the sixth dimension
- 'I AM Pure Love' in the seventh dimension'

The 'I AM' prefix sets the intention to your unconscious and the Divine that you are seeking to align with your higher self or the highest potential of your personal blueprint – the Godspark within. For a full discussion of the affirmations connected to each chakra, and additional exercises and visualisations on your chakras, please read my channelled work *Velocity Ascension*.

Archangels and Chakras

The list below summarises the main characteristics of the different Archangels that work specifically on our chakras. When we are meditating on a particular chakra we can ask that Archangel to work with us on its healing and powering. We can also ask for help from the Archangel relevant to the chakra connected to the physical challenge we are addressing.

- Sandalphon – works with the earth star chakra –Sandalphon helps us ground ourselves to Earth and manifest in the earthly plane. The Earth Star chakra is the source of our potential, so Sandalphon works with us to realise our full potential.
- Gabriel – works with the root and sacral chakras – Gabriel is the angel of purification, creativity and writers. Gabriel is also a messenger, including revealing the Quranic messages to Prophet Mohammed.
- Uriel – works with the solar plexus chakra – angel of fearlessness, or peace and harmony. Uriel commands the Angels of Peace. We need to find peace within ourselves before we can enable peace in the world. Work with Uriel to realise your full personal power for the good of the world.
- Chamuel – works with the heart chakra – she leads the angels of love, and teaches us to love unconditionally.
- Michael – works with the throat chakra – he is a Warrior Angel who leads the angels of protection. Those connected to him are strong and

he helps them show leadership, charisma, and integrity.
- Raphael – works with the third eye chakra. Raphael is the Archangel of healing. Raphael works with doctors and nurses and those pledged to help heal others through healing.
- Jophiel – works with the crown chakra – means 'Beauty of God' – angel of wisdom, insight, and illumination.
- Metatron – works with the star chakra –Metatron is the most powerful Archangel. He helps us become spiritually strong and connect to the celestial kingdom.

Appendix 3

OTHER CELESTIAL TOOLS

The Golden, Silver, Violet Flame

In recent decades, the celestial realms have bestowed on Earth a number of gifts to help us raise our vibrations and that of the Earth. One of the most powerful began with the violet flame that Archangel St Germain brought to Earth. More recently, the silver flame was added to this, and in 1964 the golden flame was brought to Earth and added to the flames of transmutation. Each flame – violet, silver, gold – is more powerful than the last, and together they are an incredible energy that we can harness.

The Golden, Silver, Violet Flame transmutes all negative energies to positive energies, releasing negative karmic patterns. We can request that St Germain or Archangel Zadkiel surround us with the flame to transmute any negative/depleting energies/thoughts coming to us or from us, to pure positive. Imagine we are standing in a pillar that completely surrounds us with this beautiful flame, and it will stop us acquiring karma, provided we are genuinely sorry for what we have done. Be very cautious, though: the flame should not be abused. If you seek to use the flame to transmute karma with the intention of harming others, it will negate the impact.

If there is someone difficult around you at work or at home, you can ask that they be completely engulfed by the GSV flame. If you are fighting a lot with your husband/wife/partner/children/friend, stand both of you in the GSV flame.

The Christ Consciousness Energy

The Christ Consciousness Energy was brought to earth by Jesus Christ, who is now an Ascended Master. It is a beautiful energy of love, and if we ask for it to be placed in our heart chakra, it can raise the vibrations of our heart and draw unconditional love and forgiveness to us.

Appendix 4

THE KAHUNAS

The Kahunas from Hawaii were wise shamans that were powerful energy healers and workers. A real kahuna is said to be able to massage for seven days with no food or water, just taking energy from the air. The Kahuna principles embody the principles that we should adhere to in reaching the 7th dimension:

Ike - **The world is what you think it is** – the ego tells you that you are not good enough, and that you must struggle and overcome others to attain what is rightfully yours, or to have purpose and be lovable. By recognising the nattering voice of your ego you can release its power and instead manifest the positive. Know that abundance flows in the universe.

Kala - **There are no limits** – the only limitations that are placed on us in terms of our life are those we place on ourselves. Once you attain the 7th dimension you understand your power to manifest for the benefit of the world and universe and for your own pure joy.

- **Energy flows where attention goes** – when we give something negative energy, the negative emotion or situation becomes amplified or more likely to occur. If we give attention to positive emotions, we amplify the possibility of wonderful positive outcomes occurring. Be careful where you put your energy.

Manawa - **Now is the moment of power** – we waste too much time worrying or regretting what we did or didn't do yesterday/last year/ten years ago. Stop. And don't waste time worrying about what might happen in the future. You have an inordinate amount of power to influence the now. Use it.

Aloha - **To love is to be happy** – with God's love you are never alone. Without giving love you are deadened, and by receiving love we experience joy. Love is the lifeblood, the joy, the healer, the flow. It is never finite, always infinite. The more you love, the more you are loved. But remember first you must love yourself (unconditionally).

Mana - **All power comes from within** – we create the reality around us. Therefore stop wasting time trying to change those around us. The only person we can change is ourself. Once we change ourselves, those around us and the situations around us change of their own accord. Know that we have total power over ourselves. Any difficult situation is merely a lesson not yet learnt, and an opportunity to learn it.

Pono - **Effectiveness is the measure of truth** - if it works it works. This is the simplest principle; it means that if we see something change around us as the result of our action, we can repeat the action. If we walk into a shop and smile at the moody shopkeeper and (s)he smiles back, the whole shop lights up. Replicate that.

Appendix 5

COLOURS AND THE ARCHANGELS

Experiment with these colours in your house, clothes and accessories. Also, invite these archangels into your home and your lives. Just say I invite Archangel [Name] into my home and my life to help me create a radiant space.

Chakra	Colour in 3rd dimension	Colour in 7th dimension	Associated Archangel	Meanings
Root	Crimson	Rose gold	Gabriel	Colour of vitality. Gives you energy, passion for life, joy, survival instinct, base health.

| Sacral | Orange | Peach gold | Gabriel | Colour of creativity and vibrant sexuality. Lifts the spirit. Warm, nurturing, good for digestion. |
| Solar Plexus | Yellow | Shimmering or sequined gold | Uriel | Power colour, colour of the sun. Use this colour to breathe in the power of the sun, the heat of the sun, the abundance of the sun's energy. Use it to feel sunshine in your life. Also helps strengthen your self-confidence. |

Heart	Green or pink	Iridescent green	Chamuel	Both colours resonate with the heart chakra in the 3rd dimension. Wear these colours in their vibrant forms, e.g. emerald or leaf green, magenta or bright or rose pink, to bring love of yourself into your life, and spread love around your home. Green also helps to feel renewed and pink to feel nurtured.
Throat	Turquoise, sky or kingfisher blue	Iridescent blue	Michael	These are powerful colours for communication and healing rifts or disagreements with people. They also help strengthen your ability to communicate your needs to others and even yourself.

Third eye	Silver or diamante	Gleaming Silver or diamante	Raphael	Add winks of crystal light to your home or in your clothes and jewellery. Adds glamour to your life, and helps you look for the 'platinum' lining in your situation.
Crown	White	Gleaming White	Jophiel	Although not strictly a colour, white is an essential part of your Happiness Colour Pot. Striking white walls or clothes help cleanse you, help you feel your life is clean, pure, helps you feel able to reach your highest path. White in the crown chakra is a connection to the spiritual aspects of the world.

| Metatron | Gold | Gleaming Gold | Star | Symbolises joy, hope, beauty, possibility, spiritual achievement. Use it to bring joy into your home and lift your spirits. |

About Helena Clare

Raised in Cornwall UK, at the foot of Bodmin moor, at aged 18, Helena took a year out from studying to teach English at a university in Kalimantan, on the Indonesian part of the rainforest island of Borneo. The experience influenced her life, both through witnessing the degradation caused by profligate logging and being exposed to the psychic abilities and experiences of the students whom she taught and who befriended her, resonating with her own ability to converse with celestial beings.

Upon her return to England she studied a Bachelor of Science in Economics at the London School of Economics and then received a scholarship to study a Masters in Environmental Economics, at University College London. After graduating with distinction she took up a joint post in Fiji, as Senior Natural Resource Advisor in the Fiji Mineral Resources Department and the South

Pacific Applied Geoscience Commission. In this role she supported governments in the Pacific to develop sustainable mineral and natural resource policies. At the same time she began training to be a Kahuna masseur, a deep spiritual massage from Hawaii, that can release emotions trapped in the body, from this life and previous lives.

After two years in the Pacific Helena returned to London and took a position with the UK government's aid department, the Department for International Development, where she spent the next twelve years. Under Clare Short's leadership the department set the benchmark for innovation and reform in the international aid and trade architecture, to be more inclusive of less well-off countries and to benefit the poorest people in the world.

After contributing to critical trade agendas including the relaxation of intellectual property rights on life savings drugs, she was posted to South Africa. Here she met her first husband and has continued her career in trade, regional economic and sustainable urban development and finding solutions for climate change challenges, designing and leading globally focused multi-million pound initiatives aimed at improving the lives of millions of the poorest people in Africa and beyond.

Whilst in South Africa she studied kinesiology, a practice that uses the body's innate knowledge to heal itself, and qualified as an Angel and Ascension Teacher with the Angel Connection School. In December 2012 Helena began channelling *The Lightseeker's Manual*.

She is mum to two beautiful boys, Tariq and Saafi, who are the delight and joy of her life. She is passionate about finding solutions to the world's most critical challenges and empowering people to find their own *highest paths*. She currently lives in South Africa with her two sons.

Free Meditation

I often check in with the Guardian Angel of each of my children when I want insight or advice as to how to support them in life or on a particular issue. This is a great meditation to help you connect too. It can also be helpful if your child is non-verbal and not able to speak for themselves.

To download your free audio meditation
"Connect With Your Child's Guardian Angel" visit
http://lightseekersway.com/sd-meditation

Acknowledgements

There are so many people to thank for this precious path I am walking with my beloved sons. I have had so many incredible supporters when Saafi has been in hospital and things have got really tough. If I start naming people I will miss someone out! So thank you to you all. You give me love every day.

With respect to this precious book, thank you to Stephanie at Authority Publishing and her wonderful team, to Renee for her interior design and Lewis for his cover design, and to all my amazing family and friends for their love and encouragement in my writing.

CONNECT ON SOCIAL MEDIA
Twitter: Helena Clare @LightseekersWay
Facebook: The Lightseeker's Way
Instagram: helenaclare.lightseekersway
Website: www.LightseekersWay.com

CONTACT HELENA
Contact Helena about speaking engagements, media appearances or just to say hello at www.LightseekersWay.com and email helena@lightseekersway.com